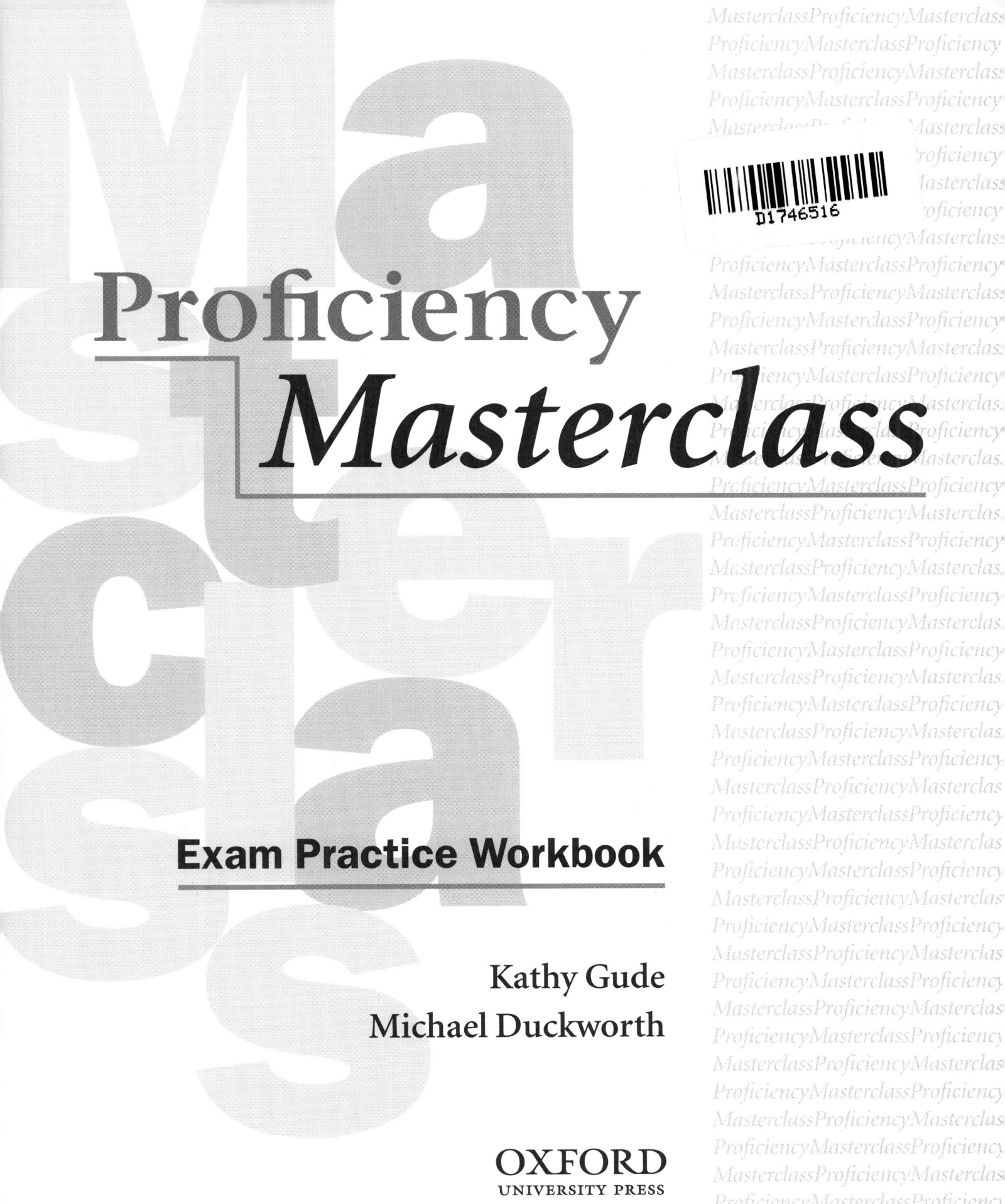

Proficiency Masterclass

Exam Practice Workbook

Kathy Gude
Michael Duckworth

OXFORD
UNIVERSITY PRESS

OXFORD
UNIVERSITY PRESS

Great Clarendon Street, Oxford OX2 6DP

Oxford University Press is a department of the University of Oxford.
It furthers the University's objective of excellence in research, scholarship,
and education by publishing worldwide in

Oxford New York

Auckland Bangkok Buenos Aires Cape Town Chennai
Dar es Salaam Delhi Hong Kong Istanbul Karachi Kolkata
Kuala Lumpur Madrid Melbourne Mexico City Mumbai Nairobi
São Paulo Shanghai Taipei Tokyo Toronto

Oxford and Oxford English are registered trade marks of
Oxford University Press in the UK and in certain other countries

© Oxford University Press 2002

The moral rights of the author have been asserted

Database right Oxford University Press (maker)

First published 2002
Second impression 2002

All rights reserved. No part of this publication may be reproduced, stored in a retrieval system, or transmitted, in any form or by any means, without the prior permission in writing of Oxford University Press (with the sole exception of photocopying carried out under the conditions stated in the paragraph headed 'Photocopying', or as expressly permitted by law, or under terms agreed with the appropriate reprographics rights organization. Enquiries concerning reproduction outside the scope of the above should be sent to the ELT Rights Department, Oxford University Press, at the address above

You must not circulate this book in any other binding or cover and you must impose this same condition on any acquirer

Photocopying

The Publisher grants permission for the photocopying of those pages marked 'photocopiable' according to the following conditions. Individual purchasers may make copies for their own use or for use by classes that they teach. School purchasers may make copies for use by staff and students, but this permission does not extend to additional schools or branches

Under no circumstances may any part of this book be photocopied for resale

Any websites referred to in this publication are in the public domain and their addresses are provided by Oxford University Press for information only. Oxford University Press disclaims any responsibility for the content.

ISBN 0 19 432929 1

Printed by Grafiasa S.A. in Portugal

Acknowledgments

The authors and publisher would like to thank Petrina Cliff, Thorkild Gantner, Lisa Hale, Chris Maynard, and the Proficiency students of St Giles College London Central.
The authors and publisher are grateful to those who have given permission to reproduce the following extracts and adaptations of copyright material:

Reproduced by permission of Guardian Newspapers Ltd:

p7 'Obsession' by David Newnham © *The Guardian*, 3 March 2001; *p8* 'Buzz words' by Richard Reeves © *The Guardian*, 8 November 2000; p12 'I feel, therefore I am' by Tim Radford © *The Guardian* 20 January 2000; *pp14–15* 'Can astrologers help you to climb the career ladder?' by Dolly Dhingra © *The Guardian* 23 April 2001; *p31* 'If we did it, so can you' © Peter Duncan, *The Observer* 22 July 2001; *p32* 'Halitosis Rex?' by Maev Kennedy © *The Guardian*, 7 Feb 2001; *p33* 'Flooded Britain?' by Robin McKie © *The Observer*, 5 Nov 2000; *p33* 'Bleak new world?' by Richard Naughton-Taylor © *The Guardian*, 8 February 2001; *p34* 'Lake Fear?' by Paul Brown © *The Guardian* 20 February 2001; *p37* 'Baby talk?' by James Meek © *The Guardian* 6 September 2001; *p40* 'Getting the balance right' by Alex Whittaker © *The Guardian*; *pp44–45* 'Terror in the heartland' by Jonathan Raban © *The Guardian* 5 October 1996; *p49* 'A toil for soil' © Daphne Lambert, *The Guardian* 7 July 2001; *p54* 'Stop or go' © Maria McHale, *The Guardian* 29 August 2001; *p55* 'Stop being paranoid, Britain's parents told' by Maureen Freely & Martin Bright © *The Observer* 11 March 2001; *p58* 'The last word on profit' © A. C Grayling, *The Guardian* 17 February 2001; *p63* 'Ghosts story' © Chris Arnot, *The Guardian* 4 July 2001; *p64* 'But The Sun can say anything it likes can't it?' by Clare Dyer © *The Guardian*, 3 April 2001; *p65* 'The rights stuff' by Clare Dyer © *The Guardian*, 3 April 2001; *p69* 'It's payback time' © Linda Jackson & Raekha Prasad, *The Guardian* 12 September 2001.

p8 Extracts from *Regeneration* by Pat Barker, Viking 1992 © Pat Barker 1992, Reproduced by permission of Penguin Books Ltd; *p17* and *p 42* Extracts from *The Oxford Companion to English Literature* edited by Margaret Drabble (2000) © Margaret Drabble and Oxford University Press 2000. Reproduced by permission; *pp18–19* Extracts from *Dream Story* by Arthur Schnitzler, translated by J.M.Q. Davies. Penguin Books 1999. © The Estate of Arthur Schnitzler, 1999. Translation © J.M.Q. Davies. Reproduced by permission of Penguin Books Ltd; *p24* 'Face to face with a Grizzly' by Kathy Cook, *Reader's Digest* May 1996. Reproduced by permission of Reader's Digest; *p24* 'A time for travel' by Kazimierz Pytko, *Kaleidoscope*, June 2001. Reproduced by permission of Business Press Sp., Poland; *p25* Extracts from *Rambling on the Road to Rome* by Peter Francis Brown. Reproduced by permission of Summersdale Publishers Ltd; *p35* 'The battle to survive – Deadly rivers of snow' by Clive Cookson, *Financial Times* 17–18 March 2001. Reproduced by permission of Financial Times Ltd; *p36* Extracts from *The Insight Guide to Great Britain*. Reproduced by permission of Insight Guides / APA Publications; *p36* 'Castaway star…' by Ben Fogel, *Hello* 29 May 2001. Reproduced by permission of Hello Ltd; *p43* Extract from *Turner's Oxford*, The Ashmolean Museum 2000. Reproduced by permission of The Ashmolean Museum; *p50* 'Horses for courses' by Simon Brook, *Livewire* June/ July 2001. Reproduced by permission of Livewire / The Illustrated London News; *p59* Information taken from CNN Traveller 2001; *p59* 'Hot Tuna' by Richard Cook, *Financial Times Weekend Magazine* 4 December 1999. Reproduced by permission of Richard Cook; *p60* Extracts taken from *The Total Package* by Thomas Hine © 1995. Reproduced by permission of Little, Brown and Company; *p61* 'Exclusive city breaks with GNER', *Livewire* December 2000 / January 2001. Reproduced by permission of Livewire / The Illustrated London News; *p62* Extracts from *More Power to You* by Connie Brow Glaser & Barbara Steinberg Smalley published by Century. Reproduced by permission of The Random House Group Ltd; *p62* 'Lost Treasure of Sumatra' by Chris Hulme, *Financial Times* 28 October 2000. Reproduced by permission of Chris Hulme; *p66* 'Prisons over two centuries' by Amy Edwards & Richard Hurley, from www.homeoffice.gov.uk. © Crown Copyright. Reproduced by permission of Her Majesty's Stationery Office; *p68* 'Ancient park under threat', *Pontefract & Castleford Express* 22 August 2001. Reproduced by permission of Pontefract & Castleford Express; *pp70–71* 'Take a high tea when you want to hit the high sea' by Bill Glenton, *Financial Times* 8–9 September 2001. Reproduced by permission of Financial Times Ltd; *p76* 'A Doctor Writes: Suspension of Belief' by Dr John Collee, *The Observer Magazine* 1999. Reproduced by permission of PFD on behalf of Dr John Collee; *pp80–81* Extracts from *Visions* by Michio Kaku. Reproduced by permission of Michio Kaku; *p82 Making the Most of Your Mind* by Tony Buzan. Reproduced by permission of Colt Books Ltd.

Although every effort has been made to trace and contact copyright holders before publication, this has not been possible in some cases. We apologize for any apparent infringement of copyright and if notified, the publisher will be pleased to rectify any errors or omissions at the earliest opportunity.

We would also like to thank the following for the permission to reproduce photographs:

Environmental Images *p87* (T.E Perry / park and ride); *p90* (Graham Burns / pond clearing); *p90* (Martin Bond / pedestrianised street); Still Pictures *p87* (Ray Pfortner / rubbish) Corbis UK Ltd *p87* (Adam Woolfitt / stone restoration); *p87* (Sandro Vannini / pigeons); Ecoscene *p90* (Angela Hampton / tree planting); *p 90* (Ian Harwood / dog loo).

The publisher is grateful to the University of Cambridge Local Examinations Syndicate for permission to reproduce material from the revised CPE handbook.

Contents

Introduction	4	Sample Speaking Test	83
CPE Examination overview	5	Answer Sheets	91
Units 1–12	7–82		

	Unit	Paper 1 Reading	Paper 2 Writing	Paper 3 Use of English	Paper 3 Summary	Paper 4 Listening	
Test 1	1	Part 1 p 7		Part 1 p 9		Part 1 p 10	
	2	Part 4 p 12		Part 2 p 16	Part 5 p 14	Part 2 p 17	
	3	Part 3 p 18	Part 1 p 20	Part 3 p 21		Part 3 p 23	
	4	Part 2 p 24	Part 2 p 28	Part 4 p 29		Part 4 p 31	Total:
	Marks:	/62 x 100 = __%	/40 x 100 = __%		/75 x 100 = __%	/28 x 100 = __%	/4 = __%
Test 2	5	Part 1 p 32		Part 1 p 34		Part 1 p 35	
	6	Part 2 p 37	Part 1 p 41	Part 2 p 42		Part 2 p 43	
	7	Part 3 p 44	Part 2 p 46	Part 3 p 47		Part 3 p 49	
	8	Part 4 p 50		Part 4 p 52	Part 5 p 54	Part 4 p 56	Total:
	Marks:	/62 x 100 = __%	/40 x 100 = __%		/75 x 100 = __%	/28 x 100 = __%	/4 = __%
Test 3	9	Part 1 p 58		Part 1 p 60		Part 1 p 61	
	10	Part 2 p 63	Part 1 p 67	Part 2 p 68		Part 2 p 69	
	11	Part 3 p 70	Part 2 p 72	Part 3 p 73		Part 3 p 75	
	12	Part 4 p 76		Part 4 p 78	Part 5 p 80	Part 4 p 82	Total:
	Marks:	/62 x 100 = __%	/40 x 100 = __%		/75 x 100 = __%	/28 x 100 = __%	/4 = __%

Fill in your marks in the boxes provided and add up your total at the end of the test.

Introduction

Proficiency Masterclass Exam Practice Workbook provides revision of the material in the Student's Book in the form of exam practice for the revised Cambridge Certificate of Proficiency in English (CPE) examination.

What does the book contain?

There are 12 units in total, each of which contains 3 or 4 full-length exam tasks which recycle the themes, vocabulary, structures and task types in the Student's Book. Each set of four units combines to provide a complete CPE practice test for Papers 1–4, making a total of three complete tests (Units 1–4, Units 5–8, and Units 9–12). At the end of the book, there is a separate section on Paper 5 Speaking. This section contains recorded extracts from sample speaking tests, with analysis, and a full Paper 5 practice test.

How can the book be used?

The material can be used in two ways: you can either work through the tasks unit by unit after completing the relevant material in the Student's Book; or you can wait until you have completed four units, then tackle a complete test (under examination conditions, if you wish), following the order of the tasks as they appear in the exam. At the end of each exam task there is a page reference to the next part of the exam paper.

Where do the texts come from?

The texts are all based on authentic materials found in newspapers, magazines, novels, reference books, radio recordings, etc.

Who is featured in the Speaking Test?

The voices you hear on the tape are not those of actors but of actual CPE students recorded while studying a Proficiency course at a language school in England.

What exam guidance is given?

Exam guidance for each exam task appears in a column alongside the main text. In Test 1 (Units 1–4), a step-by-step *Answering strategy* introduces each part of the examination. This is followed by *Question hints* on specific exam questions. Test 2 (Units 5–8) contains further specific hints covering question types not featured in Test 1. Test 3 (Units 7–12) is unguided and provides an opportunity for you to practise the papers under exam conditions, including filling in the answer sheets provided at the back of the book.

How are the tests marked?

Marks are given for each part of the test in the key provided (With Key edition only). You can record your marks for each of the exam tasks in the grid provided on the contents page and then compare your results over all three tests.

Overview of the revised Certificate of Proficiency in English examination

Paper 1   Reading (1 hour 30 minutes)
Part 1
Three short texts with 6 four-option multiple-choice cloze questions on each one.
Part 2
Four short texts with 2 four-option multiple-choice questions on each one.
Part 3
A gapped text with 7 questions.
Part 4
One long text with 7 four-option multiple-choice questions.

Test focus
The Reading paper tests the understanding of the meaning of written English at word, phrase, sentence, paragraph and whole text level.

Paper 2   Writing (2 hours)
Part 1
One compulsory question (300 to 350 words). The format of the question could be: an article, an essay, a letter or a proposal. A short text is always included as a prompt.

Part 2
One question from a choice of four, which includes one question from a choice of three set texts. The format of the question could be: an article, a letter, a proposal, a review or a report. The set text question could be in the form of: an article, an essay, a letter, a review or a report.

Test focus
The Writing paper assesses the ability to write specified task types with a range of functions.

Paper 3   Use of English (1 hour 30 minutes)
Part 1
An open cloze text with 15 questions.
Part 2
One short text with 10 word formation questions.
Part 3
Six sets of three gapped sentences.
Part 4
Eight key word transformation questions.
Part 5
Two texts with 4 comprehension questions and a summary writing task.

Test focus
The Use of English paper tests knowledge and control of grammar and vocabulary through various tasks at text and sentence level.

Paper 4   Listening (about 40 minutes)

Part 1
Four short extracts with 2 three-option multiple-choice questions on each one.
Part 2
One long text with 9 sentence completion questions on each one.
Part 3
One long text with 5 four-option multiple-choice questions.
Part 4
One long text with 6 matching questions.

Test focus
The Listening paper tests the understanding of the meaning of spoken English, the ability to extract information from a text, and the understanding of speakers' attitudes and opinions.

Paper 5   Speaking (19 minutes)

Part 1
A three-minute interview.
Part 2
A four-minute collaborative task.
Part 3
Individual two-minute long turns and a follow-up discussion. 12 minutes in total.

Test focus
Paper 5 Speaking tests the ability to produce spoken English using a range of functions to perform different tasks.

Marking
Each paper has equal weighting and represents 20 per cent of the total marks in the examination.

Test 1 Unit 1

Answering strategy

1 Read the first text to get a general understanding.
2 Read the text again carefully and look at the choice of options.
3 Try each option in the gap before making your final decision.
4 Check that the word you have chosen fits the context before and after the gap.
5 If you are unsure about an answer, leave the question and come back to it when you have completed the other items.
6 Repeat the procedure for the other texts.

Question hints

Questions in this part of the test focus on:
- vocabulary in different contexts, e.g. fixed phrases, collocations, idioms, parts of phrasal verbs and complementation (where incorrect options can be wrong for grammatical reasons).
- the meaning of a word in a particular context, e.g. linkers or complete phrasal verbs. The incorrect options may be grammatically correct but they do not fit the gap.

Q1 Complementation: only one verb follows the pattern of verb + object pronoun + infinitive.

Q2 All the phrasal verbs fit grammatically into this sentence but only one has the correct meaning in this context.

Q3 This is a fixed phrase, i.e. *on the ... of doing something*.

Paper 1 Reading   Part 1

For questions **1–18**, read the three texts below and decide which answer (**A, B, C** or **D**) best fits each gap.

Futile exercise?

Isn't it typical? For years, they have been (1) .... me to take up some regular exercise. Fortunately, I have been able to (2) .... the evil hour when I had to make a decision. And what happens when I am on the (3) .... of relenting? They double-cross me. A little but often, that's what I signed up for. No running up mountains or playing squash at lunch-time. I spent £200 on an exercise bike. Just 20 minutes of moderate (4) .... three times a week. But no sooner had I submitted to the new regime than I became aware that something was amiss. 'Twenty minutes?' said a friend when I (5) .... that I had taken ownership of my body. With a (6) .... in his eye, he added, 'I think you'll find that the necessary time per session is now 30 minutes minimum!'

1	A	wishing	B	pleading	C	urging	D	demanding
2	A	clear out	B	break up	C	put off	D	set down
3	A	spot	B	point	C	edge	D	moment
4	A	exertion	B	labour	C	employment	D	toil
5	A	foretold	B	announced	C	advertised	D	published
6	A	beam	B	light	C	flash	D	twinkle

Buzz words

Once upon a time, it was only metal that could be stressed out. Now, it seems that most workers are feeling the (7) .... . Stress is described, with a certain paradoxical exuberance, by some as a 'modern plague'; by others as weak-minded nonsense fuelled by a community of therapists and counsellors, eager to (8) .... troubled minds. Stress is in (9) .... of becoming one of those words – along with empowerment and creativity – that is made worthless through (10) .... and overuse. It is certainly the case that each (11) .... on stress seems to outdo the last – but the findings may not (12) .... a real rise in stress levels. The trouble with statistics like these is that they influence each other.

7	A	stretch	B	pull	C	strain	D	heave
8	A	soften	B	appease	C	soothe	D	compose
9	A	threat	B	danger	C	menace	D	hazard
10	A	deformity	B	contortion	C	distortion	D	perversion
11	A	inspection	B	view	C	examination	D	survey
12	A	express	B	display	C	indicate	D	designate

Question hints

Q15 Two verbs cannot be followed by *of* in the active form. One verb can never be followed by *of*.

Doing the rounds

Dr Yealland came out of his room, flanked by two junior doctors, (13) .... hands briskly with the physician he had agreed to show around the hospital and said that he thought the best general (14) .... was perhaps simply a ward round. The party (15) .... of Yealland, the two junior doctors who were being put through their paces, a ward sister, who made no (16) .... and was invited to make none, and a couple of orderlies who hovered in the background in case they were required to lift. Yealland was an impressive figure. In conversation he did not merely meet your eye, but stared so (17) .... that you felt your skull had become transparent. His speech was extremely precise. Something in this steady, unrelenting projection of (18) .... made Rivers want to laugh, but he didn't think he'd have wanted to laugh if he'd been a junior doctor or a patient.

13	A	moved	B	waved	C	touched	D	shook
14	A	acquaintance	B	presentation	C	establishment	D	introduction
15	A	comprised	B	consisted	C	composed	D	contained
16	A	repetition	B	interruption	C	contribution	D	intervention
17	A	thoughtfully	B	intently	C	diligently	D	emotionally
18	A	authority	B	weight	C	might	D	charge

Paper 1 Part 2 ➧ page 24

Paper 3 Use of English — Part 1

For questions **1–15**, read the text below and think of the word which best fits each space. Use only **one** word in each space. There is an example at the beginning **(0)**.

Answering strategy

1. Read the whole text quickly to get a general understanding.
2. Read the text again, in complete sentences, not simply line by line. Try to choose a word to complete each gap.
3. Check that the word you have chosen fits the context before and after the gap.
4. If you are unsure about an answer, leave the question and come back to it when you have completed the other items.

Question hints

Questions in this part of the test can be:
- purely grammatical.
- lexico-grammatical (a mixture of vocabulary and grammar).

Q1 This is lexico-grammatical. A phrasal verb is required, and you need to find a meaning to fit the context of the first two sentences.

Q6 This is an idiom. Only one answer is possible.

Q9 This is grammatical. A connector is needed to ensure the coherence of the sentence.

Q14 Be careful here. You need to read the complete sentence to understand what kind of word is needed.

Light up your face with gladness

Are you frowning as you read this? Habitual frowners may not even be **(0)** _aware_ that their foreheads are creased, and will need to touch their brows to **(1)** .... out. A permanent frown is forbidding and unattractive, yet it is very easy to get into the **(2)** .... of frowning. You can stop yourself by placing your hand on your forehead to check whether your brow is smooth **(3)** .... you happen to be reading or watching television. In this way, you can begin to unlearn a negative piece of body language – and if you suffer from headaches, you should find yourself suffering from them much **(4)** ....

Smiling at yourself may make you feel a **(5)** .... self-conscious – but it works! Next time you are **(6)** .... the weather, physically or emotionally, you can test for **(7)** .... the therapeutic powers of smiling. Each **(8)** .... the expression fades from your face, try again and again **(9)** .... you begin to notice an improvement in yourself. In a large number of cases, this simple technique will produce noticeable benefits **(10)** .... a short space of time – and it's free.

As **(11)** .... as cheering yourself up, smiling at someone else can help **(12)** .... of you to feel better, for a smile tends to call forth an answering smile. **(13)** .... of the reasons why we are attracted to smiling faces is because they can affect our autonomic nervous system. Facial expressions and moods are catching, **(14)** .... we are not simply registering that someone is cheerful or cross – we are experiencing the same emotion. If you are always surrounded by miserable people with long faces, you are more than **(15)** .... to suffer depressive feelings yourself eventually.

Paper 3, Part 2 ➡ page 16

Paper 4 Listening   Part 1

Answering strategy

1. Read through the initial sentence and the questions for each extract carefully but quickly (you have 15 seconds for this). This will give you an idea of what to listen for.
2. During the 5 seconds' pause between extracts, quickly re-read the statement and questions for the next extract.
3. Circle your answers while you listen.
4. If you are unsure about an answer, make a mark beside the option you think is correct, then make your final choice when you listen for the second time.

You will hear four different extracts. For questions **1–8**, choose the answer (**A**, **B** or **C**) which fits best according to what you hear. There are two questions for each extract.

Extract One

You hear a man talking about the plant lavender.

1. How does he regard lavender nowadays?
   - A   It's something grandmothers keep on dressing tables.
   - B   It's a reminder of the past.
   - C   It's become much more popular.

2. What warning does he give about buying lavender-based products?
   - A   Their smell may be too overwhelming.
   - B   They may contain artificial additives.
   - C   They may be labelled incorrectly.

Question hints

Questions in this part of the test focus on: general meaning, detail, main ideas, feelings, opinions, attitude, function, purpose and topic.

Q2 This focuses on detail. You need to listen for specific information.

Q3 You need to listen carefully to the speakers' reactions to each other's comments.

Extract Two

You hear two work colleagues talking about their eating habits.

3. What do they agree about?
   - A   the importance of working regular hours
   - B   the necessity to organise one's life
   - C   the advice given by nutrition experts

4. What do they decide to do?
   - A   skip lunch when they're busy at work
   - B   forget about conventional eating habits
   - C   treat themselves to a proper meal

Question hints

Q5 This focuses on opinion. You need to listen carefully for the speaker's own views.

Extract Three

You hear a doctor talking on a radio health programme about how to improve the quality of life.

5   In the speaker's opinion, what effect does taking up extra activities like aerobics have?

   A   It reduces our sense of failure.
   B   It increases our workload.
   C   It improves our sleep patterns.

   [5]

6   The speaker advises those under pressure to

   A   manage their time more realistically.
   B   forget about the chores they have to do.
   C   write a long list of what needs doing.

   [6]

Question hints

Q7 Look out for answers which appear correct, but may not be. *Safety* is mentioned but is there a *great emphasis* on it?

Extract Four

You hear a woman talking on a sports programme about a white-water rafting centre.

7   Why does she recommend the centre?

   A   The rapids are more challenging than on most rivers abroad.
   B   The organisers put a great emphasis on safety.
   C   The activities are suitable for newcomers to the sport.

   [7]

8   What can sometimes happen at the centre?

   A   There may not be enough guides for one-to-one tuition.
   B   There may be insufficient water to practise on.
   C   There may not be a place if you don't book well in advance.

   [8]

Paper 4, Part 2 ▶ page 17

Unit 2

Answering strategy

1. Read the text to get a general understanding.
2. Look at the first part of each question 1–7 but not the options and try to find your own answer in the text. Remember that the questions always follow the order of the text.
3. Read the four options and find one to match your own answer.
4. When you have made your choice, check again to make sure the other three options are not correct.

Paper 1 Reading   Part 4

You are going to read an article about a leading neurologist. For questions **1–7**, choose the answer (**A**, **B**, **C** or **D**) which you think fits best according to the text.

I feel, therefore I am

Antonio Damasio makes himself up as he goes along. Every waking moment, he is engaged in the study of his identity. Beyond the core self – the man who absent-mindedly picks up the orange juice or steps around the furniture – is an autobiographical fiction; he is an actor in a drama he writes for himself. At least, that's how the distinguished professor at the University of Iowa College of Medicine sees it.

The centrepiece of Damasio's exploration is the brain. It is part of the machinery of life management. It keeps the heart beating and fight-or-flight machinery prepared for danger. It tells you when you are hungry. But it can also stun you with questions like, 'What was there before time began?' Damasio is one of a world-wide brainstorm of neurologists exploring the great question of consciousness, the inexplicable mystery of why humans know who they are, where they came from and what they would really like for supper. And the key, for him, is that all human identity is a kind of fiction. We are all engaged in the process of self-creation.

Damasio was born in Portugal in 1944. From his earliest years, he was fascinated by how things worked, by engines made by Meccano. He went from there to the mechanisms of the mind, dithered about being a writer or philosopher, and then read about brain research and decided this was exactly what he wanted to do. 'I went into medical school and straight into the thing that interested me most.'

Well into his career as a neurologist – he has a chair at the Salk Institute in La Jolla, California, as well as a department in Iowa – he began to get interested in cases of frontal lobe damage. There were several cases of people who, before suffering damage of this kind, were considered honest, trustworthy and dependable, but afterwards became vulgar, irresponsible and capricious. These cases were classic pieces of evidence that personality and identity were creations of the brain, and that the brain was a machine into which spanners could be thrown. Damasio, however, was more interested in the lesson to be drawn from the way patients with this condition will take decisions.

'What people with frontal lobe damage have is an inability to decide correctly; they do it in a setting where the emotions are gone. You maintain your overt intelligence. You speak normally, you are very smart, you have lots of memory – but you make the most foolish decisions in relation to yourself, your family and your work. The big distinction is that you no longer have an ability to emote and feel normally, especially in relation to social emotions. You don't feel guilt – you don't feel pride for that matter – and so your ability to reason properly has been lost. And that is what put me on to the idea that emotion is really the only explanation for this kind of problem. All my work starts from here.'

Damasio feels that what makes human beings unique is that they feel emotions. And they don't just experience risk, danger and pain, they know they experience these things. That is the first step on the journey to consciousness and, ultimately, to the higher consciousness that – helped by a prodigious memory and fed by a fantastic capacity for language – leads to art and philosophy and the creation of conscience. Damasio thinks that conscience is one of humankind's great creations.

People ask him, 'Aren't you afraid of solving the problem of consciousness? Aren't you afraid of taking away the mystery?' He thinks not. In his opinion, consciousness itself is not a problem. The real problem is knowing that we have a mind. There is a difference between having a movie in the brain and knowing that this movie is different from someone else's. That is a problem neuroscientists might be able to solve.

Question hints

Questions in this part of the test focus on:
- content, detail or main ideas.
- opinion, implication, attitude or tone.
- purpose of the text.
- text organisation, e.g. how the writer: uses imagery; refers to other parts of the text; makes comparisons.

Q1 Option A: decide whether the text suggests that Damasio has actually lost his identity. Option B: does the text mention *several* identities?

Q3 Two options are true but they are not a correct completion of the stem. Option D: decide whether *tried unsuccessfully* matches with *dithered* in the text.

Q6 Think about the meaning of *the first step on the journey to consciousness*.

Q7 Read the stem carefully: concentrate on what Damasio says *about neuroscientists*.

---

1 In the first paragraph, the writer says that neurologist Antonio Damasio thinks of himself as

- **A** a man who has lost his identity.
- **B** a human being with several different identities.
- **C** a person searching for a path in life.
- **D** an author who is creating his own identity.

2 Damasio believes that all humans are living in

- **A** a world of unreality.
- **B** fear that they are mortal.
- **C** a state of semi-consciousness.
- **D** the knowledge that their existence is meaningless.

3 Damasio became aware of what pattern his life would take when he

- **A** began playing with engines as a child.
- **B** enrolled in medical school.
- **C** saw something which aroused his interest.
- **D** tried unsuccessfully to become a writer.

4 In paragraph 4, the writer says that after some time, Damasio began to realise that patients with frontal lobe brain damage

- **A** relied on others to look after them.
- **B** were unable to pinpoint the cause of the damage.
- **C** underwent a complete change of personality.
- **D** became depressed before coming to terms with their condition.

5 Damasio himself says that one of the most noticeable symptoms of frontal lobe damage is

- **A** an increased awareness of pain or guilt.
- **B** a tendency to become over-emotional.
- **C** a failure to make decisions quickly.
- **D** an inability to judge situations correctly.

6 What does the writer say about consciousness in the penultimate paragraph?

- **A** It increases our ability to experience risk, pain and danger.
- **B** It can improve our power of speech.
- **C** It is something that has to be acquired.
- **D** It cannot be created by humans.

7 What does Damasio say about neuroscientists in the last paragraph?

- **A** They don't like being asked awkward questions.
- **B** They know the problems consciousness creates in the mind.
- **C** They have worked out how we create pictures in our brain.
- **D** They may one day be able to understand consciousness better.

Paper 3 Use of English   Part 5

For questions **1–5**, read the following texts on astrology. For questions **1–4**, answer with a word or short phrase. You do not need to write complete sentences. For question **5**, write a summary according to the instructions given.

Answering strategy
Comprehension
1. Tackle each text separately. Do not look at the summary question at this stage.
2. Read the text through carefully before looking at the questions.
3. Read each question carefully, noting any references to paragraphs or lines in the text.
4. As far as possible, answer questions using your own words.

Question hints
Comprehension
Questions in this part of the test focus on:
- recognising and understanding the use of individual words or phrases.
- awareness of the style of writing.
- how the writer refers to other parts of the text.

Q1 Think of how the word *adrift* is normally used in context.

Q2 *Scepticism* refers to *doubting the truth of something*.

Are you adrift in the world of work? Need some direction? Career answers could lie in your zodiac, according to research by a recruitment agency. A third of job seekers interviewed felt that clues to their prospects lay in their birth charts, and 6% had seen an astrologer for career advice. More than a third of respondents felt that knowing a person's star sign could prevent office arguments. Really? And more than half regularly checked horoscopes for advice on their emotional lives. Yet only 9% said they believed what they read. So why resort to horoscopes? After all, Mystic Meg and Russell Grant surely aren't the first names to spring to mind when wondering who to turn to for professional advice? Or are they?

line 1

In order to really understand yourself, you have to have a full reading by a trained astrologer not just read your sign in a newspaper or magazine, according to a spokesperson for the recruitment agency. Astrologer and tarot reader Carolynn Townsend has been working in her field for 23 years and is keen to point out that astrology is actually a science. Indeed!

Townsend is fully aware that astrology can too easily be written off as mumbo-jumbo. 'Anyone can become an astrologer or tarot reader. That's the problem, that's why there are so many charlatans, and there are certainly some very strange tarot readers around,' she says. Anyone seeking to gain a reading should rely either on personal recommendation or otherwise check with the British Astrological and Psychic Society, advises Townsend.

1   What image does the use of the word 'adrift' (line 1) convey?

   ....

2   Which two words does the writer use to suggest the possible scepticism of both writer and reader?

   ....

Answering strategy

Summary

1. Read the question carefully so that you know exactly what you are being asked to summarise.
2. Scan each text and underline the information to include in your summary.
3. Make a list of points to include.
4. Decide the order in which to put your points.
5. Write a cohesive paragraph, using link words and connectors where appropriate.
6. Check that you have included all the necessary information and omitted nothing essential.

Question hints

Summary

Q5
- Identify the benefits of using astrology – there should be four or five points. Do not include anything which is not a benefit.
- Decide in which order the points should appear in your summary, e.g. two may be connected in some way.
- Use your own words whenever possible.
- Proofread your paragraph carefully and check the number of words you have written.

Oliver Morrish, a 24-year-old physics graduate from Kent University, heeded the advice of a friend and had a reading done by a recommended astrologer on the subject of his non-starting career. 'I had a third-class degree and wanted a job in medical physics. Everyone told me to forget it because it wasn't going to happen. I tried every career approach I could think of and wasn't getting anywhere, so I was open to an alternative perspective,' he says.

Morrish became frustrated with conventional career counsellors who had a fixed way of regarding people. 'A lot of career advisors categorise you and put you in a box, and then try and match that up with a job. But it's important to look at an individual's character traits and see what they want out of their own career. It should be about you choosing a career for yourself rather then being told what you should be,' he says.

As a scientist, Morrish says he was sceptical, but his confidence in his career choice and in himself was flagging. The consultation was a present from a friend, so he felt he had nothing to lose. 'It's not about fortune-telling. It's a way of clarifying things. I was told that my career choice was right and that I should carry on pursuing it. Since then I've found a job in the medical field,' he says. Whether it's spooky or just plain coincidence is debatable. But perhaps we, too, should consult the stars.

---

3 What phrase does the writer use in paragraph 2 to convey the idea of stereotyping?

....

4 Which word in paragraph 3 suggests that there might be something out of the ordinary about what happened to Oliver?

....

5 In a paragraph of between **50 and 70** words, summarise **in your own words as far as possible**, the benefits of astrology as mentioned in the texts.

Paper 3 Use of English   Part 2

Answering strategy

1 Read the title and the text quickly, ignoring the spaces and the words on the right.
2 Read each complete sentence where a word is missing and try to guess what part of speech the word will be.
3 Try to change the words on the right into the parts of speech you are looking for.
4 Check that each word fits into the sentence grammatically and makes sense.
5 Read the full text to check that it makes sense.

Question hints

Questions test vocabulary in context. As well as adding prefixes or suffixes, you may need to change other letters to form the word you need. Remember that the word you need may have the opposite meaning to the word in capitals.

Q1 You need to add both a prefix and a suffix to form the part of speech you need.

Q2 You need to change the meaning of this word by adding a prefix or a suffix.

Q8 You need to change letters as well as adding a suffix.

Q10 The context indicates whether this word should be positive or negative in tone.

For questions **1–10**, read the text below. Use the word given in **capitals** at the end of some of the lines to form a word that fits in the space in the same line. There is an example at the beginning **(0)**.

The mysteries of the skies

Three hundred and fifty years before the first men looked down on the (0) *amazingly* beautiful surface of the moon from close quarters, Galileo Galilei's newly built telescope (1) .... him to look at the edge of the hitherto mysterious sphere. He saw that the apparently (2) .... surface was not divinely smooth and round, but bumpy and imperfect. He realised that although the moon might appear (3) .... , resembling a still life painted by the hand of a cosmic (4) .... , it was a real world, perhaps not so very different from our own. This amounted to a great (5) .... hardly to be expected in his day and age, although nowadays his (6) .... may appear to some to be trivial and (7) ....

AMAZE
ABLE
LIVE

ACT
ART
ACHIEVE
CONCLUDE
SIGNIFY

Not long after Galileo's lunar observations, the skies which had previously been so (8) .... revealed more of their extraordinary mysteries. Casting around for further wonders, Galileo focused his lens on the (9) .... planet of Jupiter. Nestling next to it, he saw four little points of light circling the distant planet. Our moon it appeared, perhaps (10) .... in the eyes of those fearful of what the discovery might mean, was not alone!

ELUDE

STRIKE

FORTUNE

Paper 3 Part 3 ➤ page 21

Test 1 Unit 2

Paper 4 Listening   Part 2

You will hear a radio talk about the writer, H. G. Wells. For questions **1–9**, complete the sentences with a word or short phrase.

Answering strategy

1. Use the 45 seconds you are given to read through the questions carefully. Try to guess what type of information is missing, e.g. a person, place, etc.
2. As you listen, read each question quickly and try to focus on the missing information.
3. If you miss a question, go on to the next one. You can complete the missing information on the second listening.
4. Make sure your information fits into the sentence grammatically.
5. Check your work carefully for spelling mistakes. Answers must be spelt correctly.

Question hints

Questions in this part of the test focus on:
- specific information.
- stated opinion.

Q2 Listen for a word which means someone who sells something. The word you need comes before this.

Q3 *Suffer from* indicates something bad or negative. Listen for something which conveys this feeling.

Q4 Do not make a hasty choice. There may be distracting information.

Q6 Don't be tempted to guess the answer. It may be very different from what you imagine.

H. G. Wells reflected the growing interest in **[1] _____** in his novels.

Wells drew on his early career selling **[2] _____** in his subsequent writing.

While working as a **[3] _____** he suffered from illness.

He married **[4] _____** in 1895.

Wells's interest in **[5] _____** made him unusual in his field.

The hero Mr Polly finds freedom by **[6] _____** his shop.

In *Tono-Bungay*, Wells writes about the emergence of wealthy **[7] _____** as a new class in society.

His later novels were criticised for not showing as much **[8] _____** as his earlier works.

The **[9] _____** of his last novel was attributed to the circumstances in which he wrote.

Paper 4 Part 3 ▶ page 23

Test 1 Unit 2

Answering strategy

1 Read the text first to get an idea of what it is about, then read the missing paragraphs.
2 Read the paragraph before and after the first gap.
3 Look at all the options to see which one might fit the gap.
4 Repeat the procedure for each gap.
5 When you have completed the task, check to see that the extra paragraph does not fit into any of the gaps.

Question hints

Questions in this part of the test focus on:
- text organisation.
- text structure.

For each option, ask yourself questions like the following:

Option C
Think what *here too* might refer to in the text.

Option D
Try to find in the text what *to do so* refers to.

Option G
Think why he needed to look up.

Option H
Try to decide what the comment *Yes, of course* is referring to.

Unit 3

Paper 1 Reading   Part 3

You are going to read an extract from a novel. Seven paragraphs have been removed from the extract. Choose from the paragraphs **A–H** the one which fits each gap (**1–7**). There is one extra paragraph which you do not need to use.

In the interim it had become even warmer. A gentle breeze brought the scent of watery meadows and spring in the distant mountains down into the narrow street. Where to now? thought Fridolin, as though it were not at all self-evident that he should at last go home and sleep.

1

He wandered up and down the nocturnal streets, letting the light wind play about his temples, until at last, with a resolute stride, as though he had reached a long-sought goal, he entered a modest coffee-house, cosy in an old Viennese way, not particularly spacious, moderately lit and little frequented at that hour.

2

With a feeling of comfort and security, Fridolin began to leaf through them. Here and there an item caught his eye. In some Bohemian town German-language street signs had been torn down. In Constantinople there was a conference on railway-building schemes in Asia Minor, in which Lord Cranford was taking part. The firm of Benies & Weingruber had gone bankrupt.

3

He was a large, broad, almost burly fellow, youngish still, with long, wavy, fair hair already streaked with grey and a drooping moustache after the Polish fashion. He wore an open grey coat over a slightly greasy evening suit, a creased shirt with synthetic diamond buttons, a crumpled collar and a flapping white silk tie. His eyelids were red from many sleepless nights, but his blue eyes gleamed merrily.

4

And for the first time Fridolin became conscious of the fact that, as he had entered, indeed even earlier as he had approached the coffee-house, he had heard a piano playing from somewhere in the depths of the establishment. 'So that was you?' he exclaimed. 'Who else?' laughed Nachtigall.

5

'Well, when one has to provide for a wife and four children in Lemberg,' he explained. Fridolin recalled that Nachtigall had finally given up medicine after the second preliminary examination in zoology, which he had passed successfully but only after seven years. Yet he had continued for some time to hang about the hospital's dissecting room, laboratories and lecture halls, where, with his artist's shock of fair hair, his invariably crumpled collar, his fluttering once-white tie, he had been a striking, in a light-hearted sense popular, and even perhaps a beloved figure, not only among his peers but with some of the professors.

6

Payment of his dues had at some stage been taken over in turn by one or other of his more affluent colleagues. Sometimes he was also offered gifts of clothing, which he accepted willingly and with no false pride. He had already learned the rudiments of piano-playing in his home town from a pianist stranded there, and while a medical student in Vienna he simultaneously attended the Conservatory, where apparently he was regarded as a talented and promising pianist.

7

For a time he was engaged as a pianist in a suburban dancing school. Fellow students from the university and medical fraternity tried to introduce him to the better houses in the same capacity, but on such occasions he would only play what he wanted and for as long as he wanted, he would engage young ladies in conversations which were not on his part always innocently pursued, and he would drink more than he could hold. On one occasion, he played at a dance in the house of a bank manager and took it into his head to play a wild cancan while singing couplets full of innuendoes in his powerful bass voice. The bank manager rebuked him strongly.

A The son of a Jewish dram-shop owner in Poland, he had in due course reached Vienna from his home town to study medicine. From the outset, the allowance from his parents had been negligible, and in any case it had soon been revoked, but this did not prevent him continuing to appear at the get-togethers of one of the medical associations in the Riedhof to which Fridolin too belonged.

B 'Nothing could happen to me,' said Nachtigall, 'or at worst this could be my last engagement – but that may be the case regardless.' He fell silent and again looked out through the gap in the curtains.

C But here too he was not serious or industrious enough to develop his gifts systematically; and he soon contented himself with musical success only in his own circle of acquaintances, or rather with the pleasure his piano-playing gave them.

D Somehow he could not make up his mind to do so. Strange how homeless, how dejected he felt since that disagreeable encounter with the Alemannic students. Or was it since Marianne's confession? No, earlier still – indeed, ever since his evening conversation with Albertine he had been moving away from the habitual sphere of his existence, into some other remote and unfamiliar world.

E In a corner, three gentlemen were playing cards; a waiter who until then had been watching them helped Fridolin out of his fur coat, took his order, and placed magazines and evening papers before him on the table.

F 'So you're in Vienna?' cried Fridolin.
'You didn't know,' said Nachtigall in a soft Polish accent with a slight Jewish intonation. 'How come you didn't know? Considering how famous I am.' He laughed aloud good-humouredly and sat down opposite Fridolin.
'How have you managed that?' asked Fridolin.
Nachtigall laughed even more heartily. 'Didn't you hear me just now?'
'How do you mean, hear you? – Ah, I see!'

G He looked up and became conscious of someone eyeing him from the table opposite. Nachtigall? Could it be? The other man had already recognised him, and, raising both arms in a gesture of agreeable surprise, came over to him.

H Fridolin nodded. Yes, of course – that peculiarly energetic touch, those strange, somewhat haphazard yet melodious chords with the left hand had immediately seemed so familiar to him. 'So you've devoted yourself entirely to music?' he inquired.

Paper 2 Writing   Part 1

You **must** answer this question. Write your answer in **300–350** words in an appropriate style.

You work for an organisation which has been asked by the town council to evaluate ways of improving safety for cyclists and pedestrians in your area. Below are some of the comments you received while carrying out your research. Write your **proposal** for the town council outlining the changes you recommend, and explaining why these steps need to be taken.

> Outside the school gates, we often have cars speeding past at more than twice the speed limit. What we need are things like speed cameras and police checks, and, by the way, I am completely opposed to cycle lanes — the roads are far too dangerous for students to be out on.
>
> Anna Berkley
> Mother of two school-age children

> I can understand that some people want to keep cars out, but city centre businesses like mine depend on getting large numbers of customers, and don't forget that we pay the taxes and provide the jobs. If you ban cars and make pedestrianised areas, how will our customers reach us?
>
> Harry Locke
> Manager, ABC department store

Write your **proposal**.

> We want to see more use of alternative forms of transport — bicycles are not given a high enough priority. We could have more electric buses, perhaps trams as well, but we won't see any dramatic improvements in the environment unless things are done radically.
>
> Tim Hume
> Environmental campaigner

Paper 2 Part 2 ➡ page 28

Answering strategy

1. Look carefully at the kind of text that the question asks for: it will be a proposal, a letter, an article or an essay.
2. Work out exactly who the reader is. Choose a suitable style.
3. Look at all the parts of the question because there will be important information in each part. Some of the prompts may be pictures, maps or diagrams.
4. Work out a suitable structure for your text and make notes about what you will put in each paragraph. Check that you have covered all the aspects that the question mentions.
5. Do not waste time counting individual words. Instead, work out approximately how many words you write on a page and use this as a guide.
6. When you have finished, read your work carefully to check for mistakes.

A proposal:

- is a formal piece of writing for a group of colleagues, an employer or a government organisation.
- contains your suggestions and ideas about a course of action that should be taken in the future.
- should be clearly laid out. Use headings for each section and leave a line between paragraphs.

Question hints

- Begin with a brief outline of what the proposal is about.
- Use the information given to decide on the main topic areas to discuss. Write a paragraph for each with an appropriate heading.
- Combine your own ideas with the opinions given to form your arguments.
- Remember to justify your points, stressing the benefits that your recommendations would bring.
- End with a definite conclusion summarising your main recommendations.

Paper 3 Use of English   Part 3

For questions **1–6**, think of **one** word only which can be used appropriately in all three sentences. Here is an example **(0)**.

Example:

0 If you don't have enough money to phone home, you can always ……*reverse*…… the charges.

After hearing an appeal from local residents, the housing committee decided to ……*reverse*…… their decision to construct a motorway next to the town.

Be careful as you ……*reverse*…… your car out of the garage – it's a tight squeeze!

---

1 Under British ……………………, for a time, the economy flourished.

As a ……………………, I finish work at 5.30.

I can't see the point of this …………………… which says we can't cycle to school.

2 The car skidded on the ice and …………………… into a tree at the side of the road.

The football …………………… the glass in the window into a thousand pieces.

The managing director …………………… his fist down on the table in anger at the committee's decision.

3 The republic …………………… war on its neighbours on 25 June.

The accused …………………… that he was innocent of the murder.

Have you …………………… all your earnings for the previous financial year?

Answering strategy

1 Read the three sentences for each question carefully, even if you think you know the answer straight away.
2 Try to decide what kind of word you need, e.g. a noun, adjective or verb.
3 Check that the word you have chosen is the same part of speech each time.
4 If you cannot think of a suitable word, leave that question and come back to it after you have done the other questions.

Question hints

Questions in this part of the test focus on: collocations, phrasal verbs, idioms, word groups and phrases.

The missing word may have a range of meanings, or the same meaning but in three different contexts. The word is always the same part of speech.

Q1 The word you need is a noun. The meaning of the word is completely different in each sentence.

Q2 The verb *crashed* would fit sentence one. Would it be suitable for the other two sentences? If not, try to think of a similar word.

Q3 You need a verb which means 'made a formal statement' in each sentence.

Question hints

Q4 You need a noun here. The word *job* would fit the first sentence but it would not fit grammatically or make sense in the other two sentences.

4   It's the .... of a pilot to look after the welfare of his passengers.

We could go to the cinema this afternoon – I don't go on .... until seven o'clock.

You do realise that you have to pay .... on goods imported from abroad, don't you?

5   Rescuers .... six bodies from the wreckage of the ship.

The police .... all the property stolen in the robbery.

Maria .... from her illness in record time.

6   A British trade .... left this morning for China.

The new manager told the staff that his .... was to improve the company's image.

The police mounted a rescue .... to find the climbers lost in the Cairngorms.

Paper 3 Part 4 ▶ page 29

Paper 4 Listening   Part 3

You will hear an interview with Ann Quarterman, who came face to face with a grizzly bear in British Columbia. For questions **1–5**, choose the answer (**A**, **B**, **C** or **D**) which fits best according to what you hear.

Answering strategy

1 Use the minute you are given to read through the questions carefully. This will help you to know what to listen for.
2 As you listen for the first time, focus on each question and then skim-read the options.
3 Circle the option you think is correct.
4 If you can't decide, leave the question and go on to the next one. You can answer it on the second listening.
5 Check your answers on the second listening.

Question hints

Questions in this part of the test focus on: opinion, general meaning, detail, inference.

Q1 Listen carefully for the following information: how people reached the lodge; whether they had a car; what the speaker felt about the area; what part her friend played in the hike.

Q2 As you listen, turn the options into questions and ask yourself: Were they unable to walk up the hills? etc.

Q3 Don't be tempted to guess the answer or discount an option because you think it is unlikely.

Q4 Remember that part of the statement may be correct but may not answer the question, e.g. the owners of the lodge may have come to meet them but this might not have been what saved them from attack.

1   Ann was hiking to a remote ski lodge in the mountains because
    A   there was no other way to reach the location.
    B   her four-wheel drive vehicle had come off the road.
    C   she wanted to find out if the area appealed to her.
    D   she had decided to accompany her friend.

2   What problem did Ann and her friend encounter as they continued their hike?
    A   The hills they were walking through were too steep to climb.
    B   The trail they were following disappeared altogether.
    C   They had no idea how to use the bear repellent.
    D   Their protective clothing was inadequate for the conditions.

3   What precautions did they take to protect themselves from bears?
    A   They warned the bears they were in the area.
    B   They avoided areas where berries were growing.
    C   They stuck to the path through the low-lying fog.
    D   They walked above the tree line to get a better view.

4   What saved the women from being attacked by the grizzly?
    A   the unexpected arrival of the owners of the lodge
    B   their ability to keep calm in a crisis
    C   their decision to run away from the bear
    D   their recollection of some trees to hide in

5   What influenced their final decision regarding their hike?
    A   the fact that their vehicle was too far away to reach
    B   their unwillingness to walk back through the forest
    C   the realisation that Ann had injured herself quite badly in a fall
    D   their fear of retracing their steps through the meadow

Paper 4 Part 4 ▶ page 31

Answering strategy

1. Tackle each extract individually.
2. Read the extract quickly before looking at the questions.
3. Read each question, but not the options, and scan the extract again to find the information you are looking for.
4. Read the four options and find one to match your own answer.
5. Try each option to make sure that the one you have chosen is correct.

Question hints

Questions in this part of the test focus on:
- content, detail or main ideas.
- opinion, implication, attitude or tone.
- purpose of the text.
- text organisation, e.g. how the writer: uses imagery; refers to other parts of the text; makes comparisons.

Q1 Detail. Option A: was the information ridiculous in those days?

Unit 4

Paper 1 Reading   Part 2

You are going to read four extracts which are all connected in some way with travel. For questions **1–8**, choose the answer (**A, B, C** or **D**) which you think fits best according to the text.

A time for travel

'Be careful not to follow a sudden impulse and jump out after your hat which the wind has whipped from your head,' read one of the warnings in the 'Handbook for railway travellers' published in 1850. Today, it might sound absurd, but the desire to exit a speeding train was nothing extraordinary then. After all, each compartment had its own door, and fourth-class passengers usually stood in open wagons. Travel in such conditions, especially in autumn and winter, required a fair degree of perseverance.

Many people were no less afraid of travelling by train than some are today of flying. British and German scientists proved that travelling faster than 24 kilometres per hour would lead to an explosion of the lungs, and that entering a tunnel more than 60 metres long would end in suffocation from the steam engine's smoke. It was advised, therefore, that only those who had to travel by train actually do so, and even then, only under the care of a doctor. So, it's no surprise that anyone who covered a distance greater than a thousand kilometres was considered – or considered himself or herself – a hero. However, probably only those who managed to put up with two or three days on the wooden benches in second and third class deserved such an epithet.

line 47

1   What does the writer say about travel in the mid-nineteenth century?

   A   Handbooks for travellers contained ridiculous information.
   B   Certain passengers had no protection from the weather at all.
   C   Passengers often jumped off trains while they were moving.
   D   Accidents on railways were exceedingly common.

2   The writer uses the word 'epithet' (line 47) to refer to the idea that passengers who

   A   travelled any distance by train would damage their lungs.
   B   went through a train tunnel would be suffocated.
   C   travelled some distance in discomfort were heroes.
   D   journeyed over a thousand kilometres were to be admired.

Question hints

Q3 Attitude. The writer mentions different feelings. Decide which one answers the question.

Q4 Comparison. The writer makes several comments about the *Schloss*. Decide how he **really** feels about it.

Burgdorf to Konolfingen

I woke in the small hours and looked out. The sky was sparkling with stars and I drifted back into sleep, confident of a day's pleasant rambling along the Emme valley *Wanderwegs*. Swiss maps are a delight to read. They are similar to Ordnance Survey maps but show footpaths even more clearly: red *Wanderwegs* like veins coursing all over the country's physique where the going is easy, and *Bergwegs*, differentiated by broken lines, where things get tougher.

At dawn I woke to fog but that was a good sign. By eight it would lift and I would be walking through country as pretty as posters. My optimism was premature. By seven the fog had gone, but I stepped out into the smell of snow. The sky was the colour of unripe plums; pale green at the horizon darkening to faint purple directly above.

Snow was the last thing I wanted, for in two or three days Belloc's route would take me over the Brienzergrat, an 8,000-foot ridge. In summer conditions it would be no more serious than a scramble over a Lakeland fell, but the southern slope is very steep, as Belloc found, and to cross it alone in winter conditions without ice axe or crampons would be inviting trouble.

Weighed down with doubts, I wandered out of Burgdorf and finally saw the *Schloss*. *Schloss* sounds exactly right, for the word 'castle' conjures up stark towers, battlements and portcullises; whereas Burgdorf's *Schloss* had all the appeal of a kitsch Beverly Hills theme home, its leonine coat of arms emblazoned like a studio logo on its grandest tower.

3   As the writer left his accommodation that morning, he felt

    A   uneasy.

    B   depressed.

    C   confident.

    D   optimistic.

4   The writer compares the Burgdorf *Schloss* to

    A   a fortified castle.

    B   a fairy-tale tower.

    C   an elegant Beverly Hills home.

    D   a pretentiously-designed building.

Question hints

Q5 Implication. The correct answer is suggested, not directly stated in the text.

A great weekend ★★ in ★★ New York

The New York department stores are the image of the American dream. Many started out as small, not very smart, shops serving a local clientele. From these humble beginnings, they later prospered and became symbols of elegance. They are often vast labyrinths, so if you want to explore all the various departments, make sure you leave plenty of time.

Everyone agrees that if you want to get an idea of New York chic, both traditional and modern, you only need to take a walk round one of these stores. The shop windows are fabulous, and the goods are remarkably well displayed on the stands for maximum temptation! In fact, many stores often ask prominent designers and stylists to create original lines of articles for them. For some shoppers, prices may seem a little higher than elsewhere, but are still affordable to visitors when exchange rates are favourable.

The main attraction, of course, is Macy's, dubbed the 'biggest shop in the world'. It takes up a whole block to itself. The red star that is the shop's logo is a reminder of its founder's tattoo. R. H. Macy was the former captain of a whaling vessel who had changed tack and gone into business. The store has a very famous beauty products department, where you can get a facial and make-up plus free samples.

5 What does the writer imply about New York's department stores?

    A They appeal to a smart set of regular customers.

    B They are the epitome of everything that is modern in America.

    C They are not easy to find your way around in.

    D Their favourable prices will tempt customers inside.

6 What are we told about Macy's?

    A Famous customers qualify for free beauty treatment.

    B It has specific departments on different sites.

    C The shop's symbol bears some resemblance to its founder.

    D Its founder was someone with experience in a different trade.

A field trip on the Moon

For politicians, Armstrong's first sentence, spoken on 20 July, 1969, with feet firmly on airless dust, signalled the end of the USA's journey to the Moon. His second utterance: 'The dust is fine and powdery. I can kick it up loosely with my toe. It adheres in fine layers like powdered charcoal to the soles and sides of my boots,' was for the geologists and it began their voyage of understanding. When Armstrong climbed out of the hatch of the *Eagle*, the grounding in geology that he had received back on Earth had already equipped him with the equivalent of a Master's degree.

Fifteen minutes later, Aldrin would poetically describe the same scene with the words 'magnificent desolation', but for the geologists in the back room at Houston, Armstrong's technical description was more like what they wanted. Through the electronic fuzz of a primitive TV camera, the world watched two men getting used to the peculiar ease of walking in one-sixth of Earth's gravity, struggling to plant an American flag in the dust without it toppling over, and posing for the most remarkable tourist snaps ever taken. But the mission priority was to get a Moon sample back to earth. This meant that the crew couldn't go back empty-handed even if there were a sudden emergency.

7 The writer feels that the words uttered by Armstrong on the Moon were important because they

    A heralded the beginning of a further era of space travel.

    B opened up a whole new area of knowledge.

    C captured the real beauty of the surroundings.

    D confirmed the view that the Moon was desolate.

8 What practical problem does the writer say the astronauts faced on the Moon?

    A placing an object on the Moon's surface

    B adjusting the controls of their primitive TV camera

    C walking without the Earth's gravitational pull

    D taking the right kind of photographs

Paper 1 Part 3 ▶ page 18

Paper 2 Writing   Part 2

Write an answer to **one** of the questions **1–3** in this part. Write your answer in **300–350** words in an appropriate style.

Answering strategy

1. Read all the alternatives before deciding which question to answer.
2. Choose an option that you have discussed in class or read about, so that you have the necessary vocabulary resources.
3. Notice the kind of text the question asks for. Work out who the reader is and what style would be appropriate.
4. Decide on the key points and plan your paragraphs.
5. Check that your plan covers all the elements of the question.
6. When you have finished, check your work carefully for mistakes.

Note: There will always be questions about the set book in Part 2. Only attempt to answer one of these if you have studied one of the set books.

---

1   You have recently returned from a holiday that you booked through a local travel agent. You are dissatisfied with the way that the tour operator looked after you and handled your subsequent complaint. Write a letter to the travel agent explaining what went wrong and why you feel they should not use the tour operator again.

Write your **letter**.

2   An airline in-flight magazine has asked you to write about a place you know well that has changed significantly because of tourism. Write an article describing both the positive and negative aspects of tourist development in this location and outline the lessons that can be learned for the future.

Write your **article**.

3   You have recently read a novel or seen a film that was set in the future. Write a review of the book or film for a literary magazine commenting on the vision of the future that is portrayed and comparing it with the ideas about the future in other books or films.

Write your **review**.

A letter:
- will usually be relatively formal.
- does not require dates or addresses.

An article:
- is a piece of text that would appear in e.g. a newspaper or a magazine. It should interest the target reader in some way.
- can be formal or informal depending on the reader, e.g. an article for a magazine for young people should be informal.

A review:
- is a piece of writing about a book, film or play, or somewhere you have visited, e.g. a restaurant.
- can be formal or informal depending on the question and the reader.

Question hints

Q2
- Think of a suitable heading and try to attract the reader's attention in the opening paragraph.
- Benefits might include: infrastructure, employment, finding out about new cultures.
- Disadvantages could be physical, e.g. traffic and pollution, or abstract, such as changes in society.

Q3
- As this is for a literary magazine, it should be fairly formal.
- Begin with a brief outline of what the book or film is about.
- When making a comparison with other works, contrast the degree of optimism or pessimism, and look at the different ways in which societies have developed.
- Finish with an overall impression of the book or film, indicating whether you recommend it.

Paper 3 Use of English   Part 4

Answering strategy

1. Read the two sentences before you consider the key word to use in the transformation. Think carefully about the meaning of the first sentence.
2. Complete the second sentence without changing the word given. Use between three and eight words only.
3. Check that your transformed sentence is grammatically correct and makes sense in its own right.
4. Check that you have included all the information necessary from the first sentence.

Question hints

Questions in this part of the test focus on:
- vocabulary only.
- a mixture of vocabulary and grammar.

There are at least two, usually more, changes to make for each transformation.

Q1 You need an idiomatic expression which means the same as *feel superior to*. Check the preposition before *everyone else*: you may need to change it.

Q2 Be careful with the form of the verb. You need an idiomatic expression using the word *eye* which means *attract someone's attention*.

Q3 Find a two-part verb meaning *accept* and change the form of the word *offered*.

For questions **1–8**, complete the second sentence so that it has a similar meaning to the first sentence, using the word given. **Do not change the word given**. You must use between **three** and **eight** words, including the word given. Here is an example **(0)**.

Example:

0   Our tickets have been stolen!

run

Someone ....*has run off with*................... our tickets!

---

1   There's no need to feel superior to everyone else!

nose

You shouldn't .... everyone else.

2   Brian was about to blurt out my secret when I attracted his attention.

eye

Had I .... blurted out my secret.

3   Anna accepted the teaching job she had been offered.

up

Anna .... teaching job.

4   They established their business in London sixty years ago.

set

It is .... in London.

Question hints

Q5 You need the negative form of *possible* and a three-part verb meaning *tolerate*.

5 Noise is something that it is not possible for me to tolerate.

   put

   I find ………………………………………………………… noise.

6 This conference wouldn't have been possible without your organisation.

   made

   Your organisation ………………………………………………………… take place.

7 I'm sick of never being able to find any coffee in this flat!

   running

   I wish we ………………………………………………………… coffee in this flat!

8 It's a pity the manager gave us the impression that the company was doing well.

   led

   If only ………………………………………………………… that the company was doing well.

Paper 3 Part 5 ➡ page 14

Paper 4 Listening   Part 4

Answering strategy

1 Use the thirty seconds you are given to read the questions carefully.
2 Note which letter is used to represent which speaker. As you listen, quickly identify the two voices of the main speakers and match them to the letters.
3 Listen to see who makes each statement and check carefully whether both speakers agree.
4 If you are unsure of an answer, leave the question for the second listening and go on to the next question.

Question hints

Questions in this part of the test focus on:
- stated and non-stated opinion.
- agreement and disagreement.

Q1 Listen for another word which means *vital*.

Q2 Listen for a reference to a place where *expert advice* might be found.

Q4 Listen for examples of dangers abroad and at home.

Q6 Listen carefully to Mark's response.

You will hear a husband and wife, Mark and Laura, talking on a holiday programme about a global trip they took with their four children. For questions **1–6**, decide whether the opinions are expressed by only one of the speakers, or whether the speakers agree.

Write   **M**   for Mark,
          L   for Laura,
or   **B**   for Both, where they agree.

1   It is vital that all family members are committed to the idea of the trip.   [ ] 1

2   It is a good idea to seek expert advice as to what is involved.   [ ] 2

3   Travelling with the family was actually an advantage.   [ ] 3

4   There is no place which is intrinsically safer than any other.   [ ] 4

5   The journey through the Himalayas was the best part of the trip.   [ ] 5

6   The belongings we had left behind began to lose their significance as we travelled.   [ ] 6

Test 1 Unit 4

Test 2 — Unit 5

Paper 1 Reading   Part 1

For questions **1–18**, read the three texts below and decide which answer (**A, B, C** or **D**) best fits each gap.

Question hints

Q1 Three of these words would need to be followed by a preposition.

Halitosis rex

The new arrival at the Natural History Museum stopped the religious education class from St Albans in its tracks. **(1)** .... most of the more static exhibits, when Tyrannosaurus rex sensed their movements, it lashed its 10-foot tail, then **(2)** .... its head and bellowed. The model took a team of Japanese engineers three months to construct and it now **(3)** .... a height of 12 feet, about three quarters the size of a fully grown T rex. When the creature, which was temporarily installed yesterday in the front hall, is **(4)** .... to its permanent home in the dinosaur gallery, it will also smell.

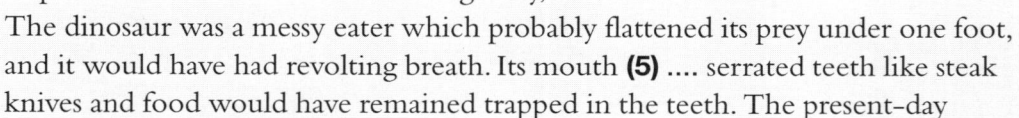

The dinosaur was a messy eater which probably flattened its prey under one foot, and it would have had revolting breath. Its mouth **(5)** .... serrated teeth like steak knives and food would have remained trapped in the teeth. The present-day model incorporates a **(6)** .... of new information about the species after important finds in the last 30 years.

1	A	Apart	B	Contrary	C	Dissimilar	D	Unlike
2	A	set up	B	threw back	C	put down	D	called on
3	A	arrives	B	makes	C	extends	D	reaches
4	A	deported	B	exported	C	transported	D	imported
5	A	included	B	contained	C	grasped	D	enclosed
6	A	wealth	B	substance	C	fullness	D	fortune

Question hints

Q12 Notice the preposition *on* in the text which should help you to make your choice.

Come rain or come shine!

The hapless citizen had only one concern: the state of the weather. Why were we constantly under **(7)** .... from gales and storms, he wanted to know? Could it possibly be **(8)** .... to the impiety of the nation? The questions were of such pressing concern that the poor amateur meteorologist **(9)** .... them carefully on a lead tablet – and then deposited it in a Roman oracle 2,400 years ago, **(10)** .... unaware that his concerns might be mirrored thousands of years later. The answers, unfortunately, are not **(11)** .... . The questions posed, however, are intriguing – for they suggest that humans have always thought that the weather is odd, and that we tend to **(12)** .... its quirks on our own behaviour.

7	A	danger	B	peril	C	threat	D	risk
8	A	according	B	due	C	resulting	D	owed
9	A	sliced	B	carved	C	slashed	D	chopped
10	A	blissfully	B	gladly	C	joyfully	D	delightedly
11	A	entered	B	minuted	C	registered	D	recorded
12	A	accuse	B	condemn	C	blame	D	fault

Question hints

Q16 Only one verb fits grammatically into this gap.

Q18 Two of these words are frequently followed by *with*. Only one has the correct meaning.

Bleak new world

A recent Ministry of Defence document paints a picture of **(13)** .... reality for the future. In an intriguing passage, it says Britain will probably become a net importer of gas over the next decade, and by 2020 could be importing as much as 90% of its needs. It also says that global warming will **(14)** .... extensive flooding of coastal areas, which could prove disastrous. Fresh water, meanwhile, will become increasingly **(15)** .... . It also **(16)** .... that if present consumption patterns continue, by 2025, two-thirds of the world's population will **(17)** .... living in 'water-stressed' conditions. Flooding, **(18)** .... with the shortage of fresh water, is likely to make matters worse.

13	A	ruthless	B	severe	C	cruel	D	grim
14	A	bring about	B	put forward	C	turn out	D	finish off
15	A	singular	B	occasional	C	infrequent	D	scarce
16	A	informs	B	warns	C	notifies	D	alerts
17	A	break out	B	come round	C	end up	D	set down
18	A	combined	B	added	C	connected	D	united

Paper 1 Part 2 ➨ page 37

Paper 3 Use of English   Part 1

For questions **1–15**, read the text below and think of the word which best fits each space. Use only **one** word in each space. There is an example at the beginning (**0**).

Question hints

Q3 Think carefully about the meaning of the whole sentence.

Q5 You need a word which means *of this type*.

Q6 You need to decide which time reference would be appropriate here.

Q14 Notice the infinitive *be* which comes after the gap.

Hannibal the giant catfish

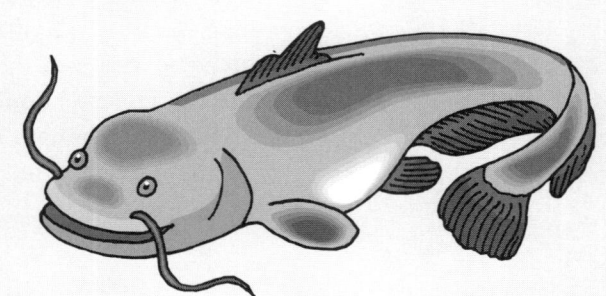

A giant catfish dubbed Hannibal the Cannibal – on (**0**) *account* of the fact that it regurgitated fish when it was caught – has been removed to stop it wrecking a West Sussex lake's ecosystem. Environment agencies confessed (**1**) .... being extremely surprised by their catch. Wels catfish are fierce predators and can eat ducks and small mammals. They are never normally found very (**2**) .... away from the warmer waters of southern Europe, and Hannibal should (**3**) .... have been there at all. Staff had been routinely netting the lake in (**4**) .... to assess fish stocks when Hannibal was caught. He weighed 15 pounds, but the European record for (**5**) .... a fish is 62 pounds. Officials feared that Hannibal would clear the 30-acre lake of fish if it reached its full potential length of 16 feet. The 57 roach and bream it had eaten just (**6**) .... it was caught compare with the average number of fish eaten by a large pike. It is believed that (**7**) .... with an unwanted pet, or an angler who relished catching the fish, which is 'extremely powerful and (**8**) .... up a hard fight', had released it (**9**) .... the lake illegally. The environment agency spokesman said the catfish had been 'wreaking havoc', chomping its way (**10**) .... fish stocks and upsetting the natural (**11**) .... of nature. Last night, Hannibal was moved to a new home in the care of the keepers of the Sea Life Centre at Brighton, (**12**) .... job it will be to feed him in the manner to (**13**) .... he has become accustomed. And for anyone out there tempted to keep a Wels catfish (**14**) .... they be lucky enough to find one, remember that the fish can only be kept on (**15**) .... that the owner has a licence.

Paper 3 Part 2 ▶ page 42

Paper 4 Listening   Part 1

You will hear four different extracts. For questions **1–8**, choose the answer (**A**, **B** or **C**) which fits best according to what you hear. There are two questions for each extract.

Question hints

Q2 Listen for the advice the speaker, not anyone else, gives.

Extract One

You hear part of a radio programme about avalanches.

1   What does the speaker say about Alpine forest trees?

   A   They can help stop a large, mountain-top avalanche.
   B   They can be swept away in a substantial avalanche.
   C   They are destroyed in large numbers by avalanches every year.

2   What advice does she give to skiers who might get caught in an avalanche?

   A   Try to find shelter before the avalanche hits.
   B   Make sure you take an airbag with you.
   C   Get rid of all your skiing equipment.

Question hints

Q4 Try not to be distracted by what the speakers disagree about later.

Extract Two

You hear two friends talking about a suburban housing development.

3   What do they disagree about initially?

   A   the need for more homes in the area
   B   the fact that young people need housing
   C   the right of property developers to make huge profits

4   Later, they both agree that

   A   peaceful protests can help build up support for a cause.
   B   we couldn't manage without builders.
   C   violence is no way to solve problems.

Question hints

Q6 The speaker mentions *bad weather*, *isolated areas* and *the longest footpath*, but gives only one piece of advice.

Extract Three

You hear part of a lecture about walking in the Peak District National Park.

5 What surprises the speaker about the area?

    A   the lack of ancient remains to be found there

    B   the absence of reminders of former struggles there

    C   the non-existence of a sign confirming public access there

6 What does the speaker advise walkers to do?

    A   avoid setting out in bad weather conditions

    B   travel with others in isolated areas

    C   think carefully before tackling the longest footpath

Question hints

Q7 Listen for a phrase which sums up how everyone felt.

Extract Four

You hear a man talking about an expedition to save the rhino in Nepal.

7 How does the speaker say everyone felt watching the tranquillising dart being fired?

    A   apprehensive

    B   excited

    C   dejected

8 What difficulty does the speaker say they had?

    A   riding on the backs of the elephants

    B   bathing the elephants in the river

    C   carrying the rhinos to the waiting transport

Paper 4 Part 2 ▶ page 43

Unit 6

Paper 1 Reading   Part 2

You are going to read four extracts which are all concerned in some way with the acquisition of knowledge. For questions **1–8**, choose the answer (**A**, **B**, **C** or **D**) which you think fits best according to the text.

Question hints

Q1 Your answer should be drawn from the text, not based on what you personally feel is true.

Baby talk

Research by scientists in Canada has revealed that the sing-song cadences of baby talk, those rhymes and rhythms and half-nonsense words that doting parents use to talk to tiny children, could be an essential step in the process of learning to speak.

The research looked at three babies with good hearing who, because their parents were deaf, had no systematic exposure to spoken words but were cooed over in sign language. The scientists found that the babies began to 'babble' with their hands at an early age, just as children born to hearing parents babble out loud. Deaf parents signing to their babies tend to use a rhythmic set of hand movements quite different from those they would use to signing adults.

One conclusion that can be drawn from this is that babies are born with an innate sensitivity to the particular kinds of rhythmic speech patterns adults use to talk to them. It seems that children are innately disposed to pick up speech rhythms from their parents and begin to babble before learning to form real words. The implication is that when parents use a special sing-song language talking to their babies, they may themselves be responding to an evolutionary impulse.

Some scientists, however, argue that babbling is nothing to do with language, and that it simply results from random opening and closing of the mouth and jaw.

1   The writer implies that parents who are deaf

    A   communicate more often with their babies than hearing parents.

    B   have babies who begin to babble at an earlier age than those of hearing parents.

    C   employ similar strategies to communicate with babies as hearing parents.

    D   prefer not to use sign language when communicating with tiny babies.

2   The writer says that research into baby talk

    A   is essential if we are to understand speech patterns of babies properly.

    B   proves conclusively that baby talk has nothing to do with language.

    C   has proved that baby talk is a response to an evolutionary impulse.

    D   suggests that babies instinctively copy the speech rhythms of parents.

Question hints

Q3 The information in some of these options may be implied but not actually stated. The question asks: *What does the writer say?*

Positive thinking

The technique for making your brain work well for you rather than against you is to apply advanced forms of positive thinking.

Negative thinking, or a negative 'mental set', quite simply and obviously programmes your brain to work against itself and you. There is also a danger, often experienced but seldom understood, that positive thinking can produce a negative result. Consider the following example: A golfer shoots into a water-hole of a certain course in three consecutive matches. Knowing about the functions of his upper and lower brain, he decides to take some positive action, and programmes himself not to go into the same water-hole next time. He spends months programming himself this way, gets to the same part of the course for the fifth time, and to his amazement and discouragement goes straight into the water-hole again.

Why? The reason lies in the subtlety of the brain, and the necessity for great care in self-programming. What the unfortunate golfer was unwittingly doing was programming both his brain and his body to concentrate almost entirely on the water-hole, rather than on his *real* goal, which was the far side. In other words, he was putting a positive on to a negative, and constantly, although unwittingly, expanding the negative. What is essential in positive thinking is to programme a positive on to a positive.

3   What does the writer say about the golfer?

   A   He always plays on the same golf course.

   B   He has some knowledge of how the brain works.

   C   He spends too long practising at the water-hole.

   D   He begins the fifth game of golf at the water-hole.

4   The writer mentions the golfer as an example of someone who

   A   takes great care in programming himself.

   B   concentrates on programming the wrong side of his brain.

   C   fails to identify the true aim of his concerted efforts.

   D   is reluctant to programme both his brain and his body.

> **Question hints**
>
> **Q5** There may be several reasons why young men went on the tour; you need to concentrate on finding the main reason.

The Grand Tour

Literally speaking, *grand tour* means 'big journey', a French phrase, because in the latter half of the eighteenth century, at the time of its flourishing, all educated people in Europe spoke French (and, if they were male, had a knowledge of Latin and often Greek). For the well-born young men setting off on their Grand Tour, it was indeed a big journey – one that would take them all round Europe and give them the opportunity to learn the nature and significance of their own cultural roots. It was a cultural search in the broadest sense. These youths were thought to be, in an age innocent of democracy, the future leaders of the country, and it was essential that they should understand their heritage as fully as possible.

They did not venture out alone, however. The Grand Tourists travelled with an entourage, prominent among whom was the tutor, the scholarly cleric whose task it was to foster the educational purposes of the journey. The Grand Tour could – and did – last for several years, involving prolonged residence in the sites of special importance. Athens was high on the list, as indeed were Rome and the major cities of Italy, from which so much of our civilisation has come. It was intended to be a serious learning process, a secular version of the pilgrimages of the religious past, and, if it seemed often to fail in this, the same comment could possibly be levelled at those very pilgrimages.

5 The writer states that the main purpose of sending young men on the Grand Tour was to

    A prepare them for positions of power.

    B enable them to learn about democratic traditions.

    C develop their linguistic abilities.

    D encourage them to experience different methods of travelling.

6 The writer implies that many of the young men who went on these Grand Tours

    A stayed away for longer than was necessary.

    B were criticised for improper behaviour.

    C were not properly supervised by their tutors.

    D did not acquire a great deal of knowledge.

Question hints

Q8 Look for a part of the text where the writer has changed his mind about something.

Managing time

Time management: two words that have me breaking out in a cold sweat. Why should I suddenly have to learn how to manage my time? Surely time had got on perfectly well for several millennia without requiring management, let alone by me. But my university tutor was adamant: time needed some managing and apparently it was up to me to do it.

First of all, let's be clear. I do have plenty of time to manage. As an arts student, I generally have 23 hours in the day that aren't given over to going to lectures. It's not as if I even have to go to lectures. But I generally need someone to tell me what I should be writing, so I go to lectures.

Perhaps I had 'taken on too much'? I'd been elected to four committees, produced a play, applied for a part-time job, hung around the college bar with my friends, and written the odd essay. But I thought I was coping well. Sure, there was the day when I did the research for an essay on the morning of deadline day and wrote it that afternoon, but that was a one-off.

On second thoughts, maybe my tutor is right. It's difficult to give up what you're involved in but perhaps it's a good idea to sit back and have a breather once in a while. Even an arts students has to get down to some real work!

7 What was the writer's initial reaction to his tutor's ultimatum?

   A He had to admit that it was sound advice.
   B He failed to see how it could help him.
   C He had no understanding of what it meant.
   D He had tried it before so he knew it would fail.

8 The writer slowly begins to realise that he should

   A spend more time with his friends.
   B end his obsession with leisure pursuits.
   C integrate more into university life.
   D apply himself to the real task in hand.

Paper 1 Part 3 ➡ page 44

Paper 2 Writing   Part 1

You **must** answer this question. Write your answer in **300–350** words in an appropriate style.

Your tutor has selected a passage from a newspaper article about international languages. You have been asked to write an **essay** giving your opinions on the points that are raised, commenting on the theoretical and practical aspects of promoting an artificial language rather than English as a global language.

An essay:
- is a formal piece of writing on a particular topic for someone like a tutor.
- is usually a balanced argument.
- should have a clear introduction and a conclusion.

Question hints
- Identify the topics raised in the question and work out a suitable plan.
- Outline these topics in your introduction.
- In separate paragraphs, discuss the advantages or disadvantages of artificial languages versus English.
- In your conclusion, answer the question clearly and sum up your main arguments.

> English comes with a heavy load of historical and political baggage, making it utterly unsuitable in many parts of the world. In addition, it is full of illogical complexities in both its grammar and spelling, which makes learning it properly an extremely time-consuming task. In view of this, it would be far better if governments around the world came to an agreement to promote an artificial language with completely regular grammar and simple phonetic spelling. This would be far more democratic and efficient, and the goal of a true international language might finally be realised.

Write your **essay**.

Paper 2 Part 2 ➡ page 46

Paper 3 Use of English   Part 2

For questions **1–10**, read the text below. Use the word given in **capitals** at the end of some of the lines to form a word that fits in the space in the same line. There is an example at the beginning **(0)**.

Question hints

Q1 You need a prefix to change this word into its correct form.

Q5 You need a negative prefix to fit the context in this sentence.

Q6 Think carefully about the meaning of the word you need here.

Q8 The word you need comes after the indefinite article but may not be a noun.

A very Welsh poet?

Dylan Marlais Thomas (1914–53) was born in South Wales, the son of the English master at Swansea Grammar School. **(0)** *Unlike* many of his Welsh-speaking contemporaries, he had no knowledge of the country's language. Thomas began to write poetry while still at school, and worked as a journalist before moving to London in 1934. His first volume of verse, **(1)** ……… *18 Poems*, appeared in the same year. He then embarked on a career in the media, spending much of his time in the **(2)** ……… popular afternoon drinking clubs of the era.

In 1937, Thomas married Caitlin Macnamara; they settled **(3)** ……… at Laugharne in Wales, returning there permanently in 1949. There were some **(4)** ……… , put forward by jealous contemporaries no doubt, that Thomas had deliberately sought obscurity, but these may well have **(5)** ……… Thomas's true motives for settling in Wales. Despite this, he gradually won an **(6)** ……… appreciative following for his writing. His worksheets, minutely laboured over and evidence of his **(7)** ……… search for perfection, reveal him as a **(8)** ……… , even obsessional, craftsman.

He enjoyed **(9)** ……… popularity as an entertainer on radio and with students. In 1950, he undertook the first of his lecture tours to the United States. Legends grew about his wild living and his **(10)** ……… habit of drinking at all hours of the day and night. Shortly before his death, he took part in a reading in New York of what was to be his most famous single work, *Under Milk Wood*.

LIKE

TITLE
INCREASE

TEMPORARY

ALLEGE

REPRESENT
DENY
RELENT
PASSION

PRECEDENT

VARY

Paper 3 Part 3 ▶ page 47

Paper 4 Listening   Part 2

You will hear someone talking about the English painter, Turner. For questions **1–9**, complete the sentences with a word or short phrase.

Question hints

Q4 The verb in the listening text is not the same as the one in the question (*proved*).

Q5 Do not be tempted to guess the answer to this question. It is very different from what you might expect.

Q9 You will need a place name to answer this question.

Turner's father decided to [__1__] in London.

Turner developed [__2__] and went to live with his uncle.

Turner's interest in [__3__] began when he was still quite young.

Copying a print of Folly Bridge in Oxford proved a [__4__] for the young artist.

Turner's signature appears on the [__5__] of the riverbank scene.

Turner's drawings of local [__6__] can be found in his 1789 sketchbook.

Turner found it difficult to [__7__] with others when he was a young teenager.

Turner imitated works by the [__8__] when he was a student.

A water-colour by Turner appeared in an exhibition at the [__9__] in 1790.

Paper 4 Part 3 ▶ page 49

Unit 7

Paper 1 Reading   Part 3

You are going to read an extract from a newspaper article. Seven paragraphs have been removed from the extract. Choose from the paragraphs **A–H** the one which fits each gap **(1–7)**. There is one extra paragraph which you do not need to use.

Question hints

Q3 Find out what *they* refers to in the paragraph after gap 3.

Q4 Decide what *the land* in the paragraph after gap 4 could refer to.

Q6 Look for a description of the *violent climate* described in the following paragraph.

From the spring of 1907 through the fall of 1908, the Chicago, Milwaukee & St Paul railroad line lumbered through the Dakotas and into Montana. From the top of any hill, one could have seen its course through the badlands: the lines of horse-drawn wagons, the heaps of broken rock for the roadbed, the debris, the gangs of labourers, engineers, surveyors. From a distance, the construction of the new line looked like a battlefield.

1

Each was a duplicate of the last. Main Street was a down-at-heel line of boxes, wood and brick, laid out on the prairie, transverse to the railroad line. The boxes housed a post office, a hotel, a saloon, a general store, a saddlery, a barbershop, a church, a bank, a schoolhouse and a jail. Beside the line, sites were staked out for the grain elevator and the stockyard. A few dilapidated shacks, and the shabby city was done. Photographed from the proper angle, with railroad workers for citizens, it could be promoted as the coming place in the New West.

2

As the railroads pushed farther west, into open range-land that grew steadily drier and steadily emptier, the rival companies clubbed together to sponsor an extraordinary body of popular literature. For the increasingly inhospitable land to be settled by the masses of people needed to sustain the advance of the railroads, it had to be made palpable. Railroad writers and illustrators were assigned to come up with a new picture of free, rich farmland – a picture so attractive that readers would commit their families and their life-savings to it, sight unseen.

3

They dangled before the reader the prospect of fantastic self-improvement, of riches going begging for the want of claimants. The terms of the Enlarged Homestead Act, passed in Congress in 1909, were generous. The size of a government homestead on 'semi-arid' land, like that of Eastern Montana, was doubled from a quarter-section to a half-section, 160 acres to 320 acres. It was an outstanding free offer by any reckoning and no homesteader could resist it.

4

The land had been granted to the family forever on April 27, 1917 under the Presidential seal of Woodrow Wilson. We had a photograph taken sometime in the late thirties. In the chemical gloaming of under-exposure stands a trim two-storey farmhouse with barns and outbuildings. We'd expected to find the place in ruins, but there wasn't so much as the ruin of a ruin in sight.

5

Our course converged with a drab-green rift of cottonwoods along O'Fallon Creek. We were lucky because that first week of June 1995 had brought perfect spring weather to the prairie – a stroke of luck, for we were seeing it as the homesteaders saw it during their first Montana spring. They arrived in a run of moist years – 1910, 1911, 1912 – and the land, in its heyday, was living up to its descriptions in the railroad pamphlets. Then the weather broke, giving the settlers the first taste of the pitiless, extreme character of the Montana climate and the winter cold.

6

Montana's violent climate came with the territory. In 1917 barely five inches of rain fell between May and August, and the harvest was disappointingly thin. Most people were baffled and frightened by the disastrous turn in the weather. They had been assured – by the government, by scientists, by the railroad literature – that this couldn't happen.

7

He agreed to rent the farm on a year-by-year basis to a young couple named Shumaker. He sold them his stock. Then Ned packed the Ford until it resembled a toppling haystack of assorted household goods, and in March that year, he and Dora sadly drove west.

A Pamphlets were distributed by railroad agents all over the US and Europe. Every mass-circulation newspaper carried exaggerated advertisements translated into many languages. They turned up in bars and barber-shops, in doctors' waiting rooms, in the carriages of the London Tube and the New York Subway.

B Following the defeated homesteaders trail, we came to a sign for a small town on the far side of the river. In close-up, the place was less attractive than it should have been – a rambling string of bungalows and trailers, with a general store, a gunshop and a dingy café.

C When stable, high-pressure Arctic air settled in over the prairie, it brought blue-sky days without a cloud to insulate the earth at night. There was almost no precipitation. With no shelter-belts of trees to divert it, the north wind raked the homesteads; whistling through every crack in their amateur carpentry, prying off their tarpaper sidings. The temperature dropped, and went on dropping: past zero, into the tens, twenties, thirties, forties. Then there was wind, fire, lightning and ice.

D As the line advanced, it flung infant cities into being every dozen miles or so. Trains needed to be loaded with freight and passengers, and it was the essential business of the railroad company to furnish its territory with customers to create instant communities of people whose lives would be dependent on the umbilical cord of the line. The company said, 'Let there be a city,' and there was a city.

E It was to see what the homesteaders had been promised that Mike Wollaston and I were looking for his grandfather Ned's homestead. We had earlier spent an hour in the wrong township, on the wrong half-section, where the US Geological Survey map appeared to have been drawn by a doodling fantasist. Now we were definitely on Ned's place but the homestead was missing.

F But the half-built new towns, in which the typical business was a single-storey shed with a two-storey *trompe-l'oeil* façade tacked on its front end, were architectural fictions. Their creators, the railroad magnates, speculatively doodling a society into existence, were like novelists.

G Rain suddenly chose to come back to the prairie in 1926. Ned Wollaston was now 54, his wife Dora was 62. They were grizzled, lonely, and undeceived by this show of kindly weather.

H We gave up and decided to tack east, then south, then east again as the road makes 90-degree turns along the section lines. One can no longer get really lost on the prairie: these roads, with their slavish devotion to the cardinal points of the compass, have converted the land into a full-scale map of itself.

Paper 1 Part 4 ▶ page 50

A report:

- is a formal piece of writing for an employer or a group of colleagues you study or work with.
- focuses mainly on factual information about the past, but should also include recommendations.
- should be clearly laid out. Use headings for each section and leave a line between paragraphs.

Question hints

Q1
- This is aimed at students, so the article should not be too formal.
- Try to catch the readers' attention at the start by having an interesting opening paragraph.

Q2
- This is aimed at other newspaper readers; a fairly formal tone would be appropriate.
- Finish with a clear conclusion summarising your views.
- Where possible, illustrate your ideas with concrete examples.

Q3
- In your introduction, outline the topic of the report and what it is based on.
- Try to analyse your experiences, not simply describe them.
- The final part of your report should summarise your conclusions.

Paper 2 Writing   Part 2

Write an answer to **one** of the questions **1–3** in this part. Write your answer in **300–350** words in an appropriate style.

1 An international student magazine is publishing a special feature about the way people's lives are influenced by family, friends and significant events. Write an article about the people or things that have had a significant impact upon your life, outlining the way in which they have shaped your personality.

Write your **article**.

2 A daily newspaper has asked readers to send in their views about whether people in rich countries do enough to help people in the developing world. Write your letter, explaining your views and suggesting what could be done to improve the current situation.

Write your **letter**.

3 An educational committee is looking into the best methods of learning foreign languages. As part of their research, they have asked you to write a report based on your experience of learning English. Write your report, explaining which factors played a part in your own studies and outlining which were successful and which were not.

Write your **report**.

Question hints

Q2 The noun you need has three completely different meanings.

Q3 The verb you need has a similar meaning but is used differently in all three contexts.

Paper 3 Use of English   Part 3

For questions **1–6**, think of **one** word only which can be used appropriately in all three sentences. Here is an example **(0)**.

Example:

0   Even the most hardened criminal is entitled to a .... fair .... trial.

The parents are dark-haired but all the children have got .... fair .... hair and blue eyes.

The weather forecast for tomorrow is .... fair .... with some scattered showers.

___

1   We were unable to .... the wedding due to a prior engagement.

The minister left the meeting suddenly to .... to some urgent business.

Would you please .... to your work and stop day-dreaming?

2   We must repair the fence in the .... behind the farmhouse.

A strong magnetic .... can be created under certain scientific conditions.

The scientist is well known in the .... of medicine.

3   When they realised they couldn't have children, they decided to .... a baby.

The government has decided to .... a firm policy towards civil disobedience.

The local Conservative party is to .... a recent recruit as its candidate to fight the next election.

Question hints

Q4 Sentence 1: Think of a word which means the opposite of what appears at the 'front' of a picture.

Q6 Read the whole of the first sentence and think of a word which completes the negative meaning.

4   The painting has an interesting …………………… of brightly coloured trees and bushes.

Although the Minister seems to have some support, many of his colleagues prefer to remain in the …………………… and keep their opinions to themselves.

Years ago, if you came from the wrong kind of …………………… , it was impossible to enter some careers.

5   The bridge …………………… after the heavy rains and was washed down river.

Ted …………………… in the office this morning and was rushed to hospital.

Resistance to the motorway …………………… after we promised to safeguard local wildlife.

6   I'm afraid we've …………………… our time on measures that no one is going to implement.

Good food is …………………… on the children: all they want to eat is burgers and chips.

Our journey has not been …………………… – at least someone is at home!

Paper 3 Part 4 ▶ page 52

Question hints

Q1 Option A: she may have read an article but you need to decide whether it was inviting donations to charity. Option B: listen carefully to see if she had cycling skills.

Q3 Listen for the **first** problem she encountered in **Spain**. There may be other problems mentioned.

Q4 The phrase *a false sense of security* is not mentioned on the tape. Listen for an expression which means the same as this.

Paper 4 Listening   Part 3

You will hear an interview with Daphne Lambert, who went on an unusual kind of cycling trip in Spain. For questions **1–5**, choose the answer (**A**, **B**, **C** or **D**) which fits best according to what you hear.

1   What motivated Daphne to participate in the cycle ride?
   - A   She read an article inviting donations to a charity.
   - B   She decided to use her cycling skills to raise money for charity.
   - C   She wanted to encourage the production of organic food in the UK.
   - D   She needed convincing of the importance of organic food in our diet.

2   What were the participants' feelings when they first met each other?
   - A   They were eager to share their doubts about the coming ride.
   - B   They felt embarrassed to admit how much training they had done.
   - C   They were optimistic about how well they would get on together.
   - D   They felt worried about being unprepared for what lay ahead.

3   What initial problem did Daphne encounter in Spain?
   - A   She was so saddle sore that she couldn't get on her bike.
   - B   She was unable to take her bike on a practice ride.
   - C   She found it extremely difficult to get off her bike.
   - D   She found the design of her bike unfamiliar.

4   What gave the cyclists a false sense of security?
   - A   the beautiful scenery
   - B   the police escort
   - C   the descent from the first summit
   - D   the height of the first hill

5   According to Daphne, the cycle ride itself was
   - A   an enchanting and magical trip.
   - B   an experience with many difficulties.
   - C   a gastronomic adventure.
   - D   a challenge no one was up to.

Paper 4 Part 4 ➡ page 56

Unit 8

Paper 1 Reading   Part 4

You are going to read an article about how to improve working relationships. For questions **1–7**, choose the answer (**A, B, C** or **D**) which you think fits best according to the text.

Horses for courses

When Ruth Redding, an account manager, was sent on a management training course to improve her relationships with her colleagues by learning how to communicate with them more effectively, instead of being asked to address her boss or her peers, she found herself talking to a horse. In fact, during the course, which is organised by Manchester University Business School, Redding found herself standing in a pen whispering to an animal and communicating in a non-aggressive way. This form of communication, which is the subject of the best-selling novel *The Horse Whisperer*, later filmed with Robert Redford in the starring role, might appear bizarre on a stud farm let alone a management training course. But horse whispering is among a number of unusual activities now being used to teach staff about every aspect of working life, from self-confidence to communication.

In the 1980s and 1990s, it became fashionable to dump executives on a remote mountainside, or windswept Scottish isle, and leave them to survive a weekend in order to develop initiative, build team spirit and promote leadership skills. An alternative to the classic 'chalk and talk' format, with lecturer and obedient staff seated round a table, it all seemed wild and rather outlandish.

Today, by comparison, it looks increasingly tame. A new generation of management training gurus are adopting a different approach. In Italy, stressed executives have been dressing up as gladiators to confront each other as their ancient forebears did, and in America, sales-people are herding cattle, while in Britain, one supermarket reportedly put its executives in Native American teepees for a weekend to develop a spirit of co-operation. Naturally, the originators of these new courses claim to have respectable psychological theories to back them up.

Tudor Rickards, a professor at Manchester, was intrigued when he heard about the work done by the famous horse whisperer, Monty Roberts. 'The idea is that instead of "breaking" the horse, you co-operate with it. Traditionally, you would coax a horse into a box and then reward it by slamming the door shut. Monty leads the horse in and out of the box and offers it a reward,' explains Professor Rickards. 'Monty's approach is founded on the recognition of a foal's instinctive desire to be part of the herd.' He matched this with research from the Industrial Society, which revealed that often the difference between a successful and unsuccessful leader is trust. 'As they observe the way horses react to certain behaviour, participants think about how they themselves or other colleagues react to different management styles,' explains Professor Rickards. 'The discussion often leads to one about experiences of bullying and abusive behaviour, a discussion that might not otherwise surface in a leadership course. We've found this helps the participants draw fine distinctions between being tough, being assertive, being supportive and being soft.'

Team building is also the aim of murder mystery days run by a company called Corporate Pursuits. Actors mingle with participants and play out a scene until someone is found 'murdered'. Clues, such as photographs, personal items or a cryptic message, are arranged around the room, and small teams, often pitted against each other, will work to solve the mystery under the gaze of trained observers.

Although fun and a sense of release is important, managing director Mandie Chester-Bristow admits that this type of corporate Cluedo occasionally meets with scepticism among clients. 'On one occasion, people were messing around and not taking it seriously at all, so I had to say to them, "You're behaving like a bunch of school children."' Another challenge can be reporting the observers' findings. 'We would never say, "You've failed," if they didn't identify the murderer correctly. Instead, we would praise them for the progress they made and how they worked together as a team.'

'There are lots of gimmicks in training and headline-grabbing courses at the moment, but what they deliver is often variable,' says Nick Isles of the Industrial Society. 'People often say afterwards that they enjoyed the event, but it's very difficult to measure how much they've actually learned from it.' He argues that ongoing training in the work place, or courses that last months, are a better way of improving aspects of business such as productivity and customer service.

Question hints

Q2 Think carefully about the meaning of each adjective before trying to answer the question.

Q3 The word *imply* in the question means that the information you are looking for is not directly stated.

Q4 and Q5 Read the text carefully to distinguish between Monty Roberts's ideas, any research already done, and Rickards's own research.

1   In the first paragraph, what does the writer say about the technique Ruth Redding found herself practising?

   A   It is a way of learning how to address your boss properly.
   B   It is based on a technique which first appeared in a film.
   C   It is perfectly acceptable in its original context.
   D   It is becoming more popular despite its eccentricity.

2   According to the writer, management training techniques in the late 1900s were regarded as

   A   undesirable.
   B   innovative.
   C   effective.
   D   demoralising.

3   What does the writer imply about modern management training schemes in the third paragraph?

   A   They have a tendency to be more exciting.
   B   Their content can actually create stress.
   C   Their creators are convinced of their effectiveness.
   D   They were developed in a spirit of co-operation.

4   Rickards found Monty Roberts's ideas interesting because Roberts had

   A   based his methods on traditional horse-training techniques.
   B   recognised the importance of developing bonding techniques.
   C   dispensed with the idea of rewarding the horse he was training.
   D   worked tirelessly with others to come up with a new theory.

5   Research carried out by Rickards and the Industrial Society showed that

   A   course discussions sometimes resulted in frank exchanges of opinion.
   B   course participants reacted negatively to different management styles.
   C   participants became less supportive of one another as the courses progressed.
   D   the bonds of trust between course participants and horses became stronger.

6   What comment does Mandie Chester-Bristow make about course participants in paragraph 6?

   A   They enjoy indulging in games they played in their childhood.
   B   Those who 'lose' the game feel they have underachieved.
   C   They sometimes need convincing of the value of the activities.
   D   They are happy in the knowledge that they are being freed from stress.

7   What is Nick Isles's opinion of the new-style training courses?

   A   Their quality is always consistent.
   B   Their effectiveness is quantifiable.
   C   Alternative courses can be more efficient.
   D   Alternative courses are more easily set up.

Question hints

Q1 Think about how to make the change from *unusual* to *accustomed*.

Q2 You need a phrasal verb here.

Paper 3 Use of English   Part 4

For questions **1–8**, complete the second sentence so that it has a similar meaning to the first sentence, using the word given. **Do not change the word given.** You must use between **three** and **eight** words, including the word given. Here is an example **(0)**.

Example:

0   They have arrested the thief who tried to break into our house.

   for

   The thief ....*was arrested for trying to*................ break into our house.

---

1   It is unusual to see graffiti in this part of the town.

   accustomed

   We .... in this part of town.

2   I am sure the robbery was nothing to do with my son.

   mixed

   My son .... the robbery, I can assure you.

3   Everything turned out all right in the end, despite some initial problems.

   place

   Despite some initial problems, ... eventually.

4   Their marriage failed probably because of their incompatibility.

   down

   The .... their incompatibility.

Test 2   Unit 8

Question hints

Q5 Think about a structure which begins *The more ...* .

Q7 Decide what *amiss* might mean, then think of a verb which is used with this word.

5 Good working relations depend on effective management.

   more

   The .... the working relations will be.

6 Someone rang the police with information about an impending robbery.

   tipped

   The .... about an impending robbery.

7 Paul meant well so you mustn't be offended by his comments.

   amiss

   Please .... because he meant well.

8 Success will come if you adopt a more serious approach to your work.

   seriously

   You need to .... you want to succeed.

Paper 3 Part 5 ▶ page 54

Paper 3 Use of English Part 5

Question hints

Comprehension

Q1 Think in what context the words *haul in* are normally used.

Q2 You may have to look back to another sentence to see what this might refer to.

For questions **1–5**, read the following texts on parents and children. For questions **1–4**, answer with a word or short phrase. You do not need to write complete sentences. For question **5**, write a summary according to the instructions given.

Contracts of Behaviour were created by Paul Dunn, a community police officer, after the police had failed to make any positive impression on a tough housing estate dominated by drug dealers. Dunn says: 'We were not successful in building up any relationship on the estate because no one trusted the police and we found it difficult to get the kind of hard evidence we needed.'

He came up with the idea of forcing young trouble-makers to mend their ways by devising a simple 'contract', setting out a series of rules that they and their parents have to agree to abide by.

In partnership with the housing department, the team identified youthful ringleaders responsible for trouble on the estate. Dunn started hauling them in for interview with their parents present. Most of the parents were unaware of the trouble their children were getting into, and would not believe the allegations until the youngsters themselves admitted what they had been doing.

When the children agreed to stop their activities, Dunn suggested a six-month contract be drawn up and signed to ensure there was a deterrent. The problem was that a lot of these kids didn't mind being arrested. It enhanced their status among their peers.

Many parents were reluctant to sign the contract, claiming they could not control their offspring. When it was pointed out that they could be evicted from their home, or in the case of owner occupiers, an injunction or curfew could be issued if their children did not comply, the parents changed their minds about doing so.

line 18

line 3

1   Explain in your own words why the writer has chosen to use the expression 'hauling them in' in line 18.

   ....

2   What exactly does the phrase 'doing so' (line 38) refer to?

   ....

Question hints

Comprehension

Q4 You need to look for contradictory statements.

Summary

Q5 There are five points to include in your summary.

A controversial new book on child-rearing to be published this week will urge parents to let their children take more risks and stop panicking about the apparent dangers all around them.

The book's author, Frank Furedi, argues that children are introduced to the culture of fear from the moment they are born. This begins with new measures to guard against hospital babynappers. Arriving home, they are then surrounded by an army of midwives, health visitors and doctors. Parents then hem themselves in even more by buying childcare books.

line 17 Furedi is apparently also concerned about the mixed messages in the news, which can easily confuse parents. 'One day a national charity will be castigating parents for turning their children into couch potatoes; the next, it will announce that letting children play outdoors on their own is a form of child abuse,' he says.

According to *Paranoid Parenting*, it is cruel to keep children inside. They need room to explore the world around them, they need time to make their own friendships in their own way without an army of adults monitoring their every movement.

Critics of Furedi argue that he is simply giving parents more to worry about. Columnist Catherine Bennett quoted Furedi's concern that playground areas are now covered with rubber to limit the damage when a child falls. 'Should they, perhaps, be constructed from something more challenging: shards of broken glass, say, or the traditional grit that was once so successful at lacerating young knees?' she wrote.

---

3 Which phrase in paragraph 2 captures the restrictions placed on parents in bringing up their children?

....

4 What are the 'mixed messages' referred to in line 17?

....

5 In a paragraph of between **50 and 70** words, summarise **in your own words as far as possible**, the attitudes of parents towards their children as outlined in the texts.

Question hints

Q1 The speakers may not actually mention *new undergraduates* or *strangers*.

Q4 Listen carefully for who gives a warning about doing this.

Q6 Ask yourself what *lead to friction* means. Decide if it sounds positive or negative. Listen carefully to find out who feels this way about rented accommodation.

Paper 4 Listening   Part 4

You will hear two university students, Harry and Natalie, talking on the radio about meeting people at university. For questions **1–6**, decide whether the opinions are expressed by only one of the speakers, or whether the speakers agree.

Write   **H**   for Harry,
           N   for Natalie,
or   **B**   for Both, where they agree.

1   New undergraduates often find themselves surrounded by strangers.   [ ] **1**

2   It is important to equip yourself with social niceties.   [ ] **2**

3   It is advisable to join in organised group activities.   [ ] **3**

4   It is inadvisable to become involved with too many clubs or activities.   [ ] **4**

5   Team sports can assist the process of making friends.   [ ] **5**

6   Living in rented accommodation can lead to friction.   [ ] **6**

Test your knowledge!

Before you begin Test 3, do this test to see how well you have remembered the answering strategies and hints for each paper.

Reading ✓ ✗

1. In Part 1, read all three texts before answering the questions. (Answer: page 7)
2. In Part 1, an option may seem correct but you need to check if it fits grammatically into the sentence. (Answer: page 7)
3. In Part 2, deal with each text individually. (Answer: page 24)
4. In Part 2, try to answer the questions before looking at the options. (Answer: page 24)
5. In Part 3, questions focus only on text organisation. (Answer: page 18)
6. In Part 3, read the paragraph before and after the gaps carefully. (Answer: page 18)
7. In Part 4, read the questions before you read the text. (Answer: page 12)
8. In Part 4, the questions do not always follow the order of the text. (Answer: page 12)

Writing ✓ ✗

9. In Part 1, you will only be asked to write either a proposal or a letter. (Answer: page 20)
10. In Part 1, it is important to choose a style suitable for the intended reader. (Answer: page 20)
11. Using headings will help you to lay out a proposal clearly. (Answer: page 20)
12. In Part 2, you must answer a question on the set book. (Answer: page 28)
13. It is not necessary to write dates or addresses on letters. (Answer: page 28)
14. An article can be formal or informal depending on the intended reader. (Answer: page 28)
15. A review should always be written in a formal style. (Answer: page 28)

Use of English ✓ ✗

16. Part 1 questions focus only on vocabulary. (Answer: page 9)
17. In Part 1, read the text carefully sentence by sentence. (Answer: page 9)
18. In Part 2, read each complete sentence before trying to find the correct part of speech. (Answer: page 16)
19. The words you need in Part 2 may have the opposite meaning to the words in capitals. (Answer: page 16)
20. In Part 3, the missing word may have the same or different meanings. (Answer: page 21)
21. In Part 3, the missing word could be a different part of speech in each sentence. (Answer: page 21)
22. In Part 4, you must use between 5 and 8 words. (Answer: page 29)
23. In Part 4, you must not change the word you are given. (Answer: page 29)
24. In Part 5, read both texts before answering the comprehension questions. (Answer: page 14)
25. In Part 5, try to use your own words when appropriate in the summary. (Answer: page 15)

Listening ✓ ✗

26. In Part 1, during the 5-second pause between extracts, quickly reread the questions for the next extract. (Answer: page 10)
27. In Part 2, if you miss a question, try to guess the answer. (Answer: page 17)
28. Correct spelling is not essential in Part 2. (Answer: page 17)
29. Questions in Part 3 focus on opinion, general meaning, detail and inference. (Answer: page 23)
30. In Part 3, if you cannot answer a question, leave it and go on to the next one. (Answer: page 23)
31. Questions in Part 4 focus only on agreement and disagreement. (Answer: page 31)
32. In Part 4, quickly try to match the letters with the speakers' voices. (Answer: page 31)

Test 3 — Unit 9

Paper 1 Reading   Part 1

For questions **1–18**, read the three texts below and decide which answer (**A, B, C** or **D**) best fits each gap. Mark your answers **on the separate answer sheet**.

The last word on profit

If you perform a service or **(1)** .... a commodity for others, you should be **(2)** .... for your pains. So much is only fair and right. If you do it well, you deserve to **(3)** .... from it. There is nothing in itself **(4)** .... with wealth, nor with any individual or company growing rich. Profit is an enabler because it takes people and peoples beyond subsistence levels to the amenities of life, to comfort and culture, to new knowledge and new possibilities. But the picture changes when profits are **(5)** .... out of others' loss or suffering. That, unfortunately, happens far too often. It seems that one well-known oil company becomes over £300 richer every second. Amazing, but not as disquieting as the fact that the chairman of a major company can earn as much in a year as 50 or 100 nurses do. Defenders of high-flying business people point out that they have responsible jobs, producing wealth which, indirectly through taxation helps pay nurses' wages. But is the chairman of a business **(6)** .... 50 nurses?

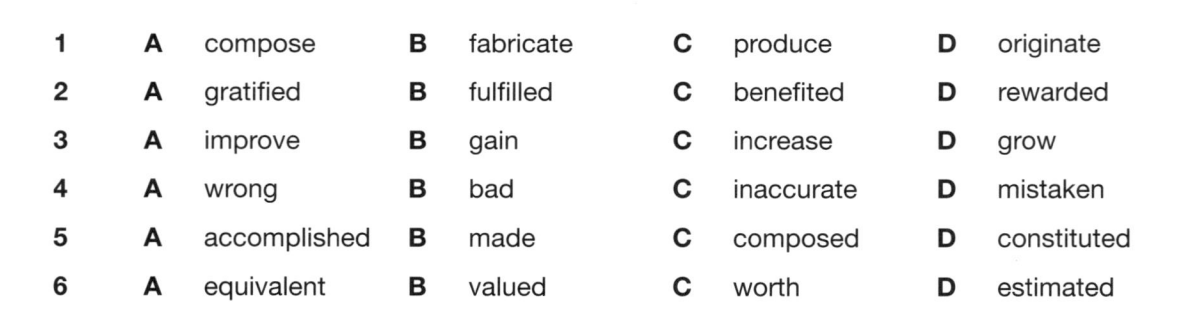

1	A	compose	B	fabricate	C	produce	D	originate
2	A	gratified	B	fulfilled	C	benefited	D	rewarded
3	A	improve	B	gain	C	increase	D	grow
4	A	wrong	B	bad	C	inaccurate	D	mistaken
5	A	accomplished	B	made	C	composed	D	constituted
6	A	equivalent	B	valued	C	worth	D	estimated

The chef's garden

One day in the later 1980s, disaster **(7)** .... Lee Jones's family farm. Hail in the middle of July wiped out almost everything **(8)** .... to the harvest season. Devastated and **(9)** .... , they decided to start again, selling the five acres of produce they had managed to save at the local farmer's market. Times were hard, but everything changed one day at the market when Lee Jones was **(10)** .... by a chef who wanted zucchini blossoms. 'I said: "Ma'am, you don't eat the flowers. You eat the zucchini,"' he recalls. Two weeks later, the chef came back, willing to pay 50 cents a piece for the flowers. 'How many do you want?' Lee asked. Word **(11)** .... quickly that farmer Jones was the grower to call for speciality product requests. Demand **(12)** .... and the family decided to give the speciality market a serious try. Today, the Joneses employ 70 people and operate a successful niche market firm with 2,500 chefs from all over the country as clients.

7	A	attacked	B	struck	C	affected	D	beat
8	A	earlier	B	former	C	prior	D	previous
9	A	burst	B	collapsed	C	spent	D	broke
10	A	undertaken	B	proposed	C	approached	D	applied
11	A	spread	B	expanded	C	broadened	D	extended
12	A	arose	B	sprang	C	enlarged	D	grew

Hot tuna

They may just look like any other dead fish, but to the merchants who eagerly patrol Tokyo's fish market, they could be the means of making themselves a small **(13)** .... . Since the International Tribunal for the Law of the Sea ordered a curb on catches of the **(14)** .... southern bluefin tuna, the price commanded by this oversized delicacy has **(15)** .... . The fish can grow to half a tonne or more, which at today's **(16)** .... means that each of these magnificent beasts could **(17)** .... an average of $15,000. Indeed a record price for a single bluefin tuna at auction has been set at a shade above a truly astonishing $40,000. Japan already catches more than half of the global annual catch of bluefin. What it doesn't catch itself, it imports. Such is the **(18)** .... from Tokyo's top sushi chefs for this tuna. It melts in the mouth, apparently, though costing what it does, it probably ought to.

13	A	wealth	B	fortune	C	property	D	prosperity
14	A	desired	B	honoured	C	prized	D	regarded
15	A	raised	B	soared	C	leapt	D	towered
16	A	charges	B	costs	C	expenses	D	prices
17	A	obtain	B	retrieve	C	fetch	D	elicit
18	A	requirement	B	claim	C	request	D	demand

Paper 3 Use of English   Part 1

For questions **1–15**, read the text below and think of the word which best fits each space. Use only **one** word in each space. There is an example at the beginning **(0)**. Write your answers **in CAPITAL LETTERS on the separate answer sheet**.

Example: | 0 | A | S |

CRAFTY PACKAGING

During what could be described **(0)** ...as... a typical 30-minute supermarket shopping trip, thousands of products will vie for your attention. Ultimately, many will make you believe they are worth picking off the shelves. How, you may ask, is this brought **(1)** .... ? The answer is by packaging – the silent but persuasive salesman.

Louis Cheskin, **(2)** .... research into the psychology of marketing began in the 1930s, was a pioneering specialist in the field. He placed identical products in two different packages, one emblazoned with circles, the **(3)** .... with triangles. He then asked people which products they preferred, and why. Amazingly, **(4)** .... fewer than 80 per cent chose the products in the box with the circles. They believed the content would be of higher quality.

'After 1,000 interviews, I had to accept the fact that the **(5)** .... of consumers transferred the sensation from the container to its contents,' Cheskin admitted later. And there was **(6)** .... surprise: even after trying out these identical products, people overwhelmingly preferred **(7)** .... in the package with the circles. Cheskin also found, for instance, that the look of a packet has an enormous impact on **(8)** .... biscuits taste. Cheskin called this phenomenon 'sensation transference'. It became the foundation not **(9)** .... of his career as a consultant to companies **(10)** .... Procter & Gamble, but of much of the research done since then.

(11) .... increasing consumer sophistication, Cheskin's original concept still works. One recent experiment involved an underarm deodorant posted in packaging of three different colour schemes to a test group. The group was told that three different formulations were **(12)** .... consideration, and was asked to judge them.

Results: one was considered just right, one to be strong-smelling but not very effective, and one threatening. Yet all three deodorants were exactly the **(13)** ....

One leading firm designs packaging for products that do not yet exist. The packaging is then tested and the marketing concept refined. Only **(14)** .... it's clear that the company has a winner will it **(15)** .... to the expense of actually developing the product.

Paper 3 Part 2 ➔ page 68

Paper 4 Listening   Part 1

You will hear four different extracts. For questions **1–8**, choose the answer (**A**, **B** or **C**) which fits best according to what you hear. There are two questions for each extract.

Extract One

You hear someone advertising a railway company's short holiday breaks.

1   What is the attraction of the railway company's promotion?

    A   the rural location of the hotels available

    B   the permanent availability of the breaks on offer

    C   the discounted extras available with the rail tickets

2   What is the company offering customers for a limited period only?

    A   discounted rates in excellent city hotels

    B   additional benefits for customers travelling in groups

    C   cheaper inter-city travel throughout the country

Extract Two

You hear two friends talking about buying works of art.

3   What do they disagree about?

    A   the price buyers should pay for a painting

    B   the effects of supply and demand

    C   what caused the death of an artist

4   What does the man say motivates people to buy famous paintings?

    A   the beauty of such works of art

    B   the pleasure of showing them to others

    C   the desire to acquire material goods

Extract Three

You hear part of a radio programme about how to sell yourself to others.

5   What did the woman's friend consider to be a priority in her job interview?

    A   enthusiasm

    B   punctuality

    C   appearance

6   In the woman's opinion, prospective employers always

    A   form positive impressions of interviewees they've already met.

    B   judge the interviewees by comparing them with themselves.

    C   draw conclusions from their initial appraisals of interviewees.

Extract Four

You hear part of a lecture about selling treasure from shipwrecks.

7   According to the speaker, why was the auction of the Dutch ship's cargo so well-attended?

    A   The man who salvaged the treasures was already well-known.

    B   It was the first auction of its kind to be held.

    C   The ship's story captured people's imagination.

8   What does the speaker say about the ship the *Tek Sing*?

    A   It proved impossible to raise the ship from the seabed.

    B   The treasures on board the ship were virtually undamaged.

    C   Buyers from all over the world flocked to Germany to bid for its cargo.

Paper 4 Part 2 ▶ page 69

Unit 10

Paper 1 Reading   Part 2

You are going to read four extracts which are all concerned in some way with human rights. For questions **1–8**, choose the answer (**A, B, C** or **D**) which you think fits best according to the text. Mark your answers **on the separate answer sheet**.

Ghost story

It was over 20 years ago that Lynval Golding helped a band to play one of the most politically pertinent singles in British pop music history. The band was the Specials and their timing was spot on. 'Ghost Town' hit number one on July 4, 1981, during the week that mainland Britain experienced what was then its worst civil disorder since 1945.

'No jobs to be found in this country ... People getting angry ...' The lyrics by Jerry Dammers had resonances amid the blazing buildings and the brick-littered streets of Brixton and Toxteth, Moss Side and Handsworth – major centres of black population in Britain's big cities.

A fifth of a century on from 'Ghost Town', Golding seems well qualified to talk about racist attitudes – what's changed and what hasn't – on both sides of the Atlantic. After all, he is a British citizen, originally from Jamaica, who has toured extensively in the US. Four years ago, he settled permanently in Seattle, the cosmopolitan port near the Canadian border which is home to his wife, June, whom he describes as 'white with a dash of Native American'. While she works in the office of a trucking company, Golding looks after their two-year-old son, Dominic.

When I last spoke to Golding in 1998, he was taking a brief break from touring in the US with other former members of bands who once recorded on the 2-Tone label. Their blend of reggae and punk has a cult following in North America, particularly among students. Golding was exhausted, but elated by their audiences' youthful enthusiasm. 'There's none of the hassle we used to get when we started,' he said. 'The crowds are much more racially mixed than they were. We've moved on a bit in two decades.'

1   What does the writer say about the band called the Specials?

    A   Their ideas were ahead of their time.

    B   Their single arrived on the pop scene at the right time.

    C   Their lyrics were inappropriate for conditions in Britain at that time.

    D   They continue to be successful against all odds.

2   How does the writer say Golding felt about the audiences he played to in 1998?

    A   He was disappointed they were not more enthusiastic.

    B   He regretted the fact that more students did not attend his gigs.

    C   He was delighted that some were fans from 20 years before.

    D   He was excited by their commitment and diversity.

Tabloids in a tizzy

Celebrity supermodels have been known to launch counter-attacks on newspapers which feed their desire for fame, but the likes of Naomi Campbell brandishing Britain's emerging privacy laws could soon turn out to be the least of the tabloids' worries. Campbell, who is furious over a story about her sortie to a Narcotics Anonymous meeting, joins Michael Douglas and Catherine Zeta-Jones – narked over the publication of snatched photos of their wedding in Hello! magazine – in the list of celebs invoking the Human Rights Act to defend their right to a private life. But now a new weapon has emerged which threatens not just to spike a few intrusive exposés, but to change the face of tabloid journalism. If it succeeds, a judge was told in a private hearing this month, it will turn our national newspapers into children's comic books.

A judgement delivered last week to no publicity at Lambeth county court in south London caught newspaper executives on the hop and sent them scurrying to media lawyers for urgent advice. The senior judge at Lambeth, Judge Roger Cox, ruled that inflammatory and strident newspaper articles can amount to harassment, giving their victims the right to sue under the Protection Against Harassment Act 1997.

---

3 The writer uses Naomi Campbell as an example of someone

  A who is unwilling to use the tabloids to her advantage.

  B whose actions have delighted the tabloids over the years.

  C who has a great number of friends in high places.

  D whose actions appear less significant in the light of current events.

4 What does the writer say about the Lambeth judge's ruling?

  A It cannot guarantee privacy for those in the public eye.

  B It will be turned into an advantage by the national newspapers.

  C It could change the way events are reported in newspapers.

  D It might lead to an increase in invasions of privacy.

The rights stuff

Who would have predicted, when the long-awaited Human Rights Act came into force six months ago, that it would rescue a £750,000 house condemned as 'the most flagrant breach of planning permission' from the bulldozers?

Councils around the country were stunned last month when Ken and Jacky Duffy won their appeal against New Forest District Council's order to demolish their newly built house, erected at twice the size allowed by the Council in one of England's prime beauty spots. The inspector who dealt with the appeal, Howard Russon, agreed that the huge structure 'seriously harmed the character and appearance of this vulnerable rural area'. He had no doubt that allowing it to stay 'undermined the objectives of local planning policies aimed at protecting the very special landscape of this part of the New Forest'. But the couple and their three young children would be homeless and possibly bankrupt if the house had to be bulldozed. Russon concluded that this would violate the family's rights under article 8 of the European Convention on Human Rights, the right to private and family life, and allowed their appeal.

When the Human Rights Act came into force on 2 October, making the European Convention part of English law, it was foreseeable that prisoners, asylum seekers and people charged with criminal offences would leap on the bandwagon. Scaremongering predictions of chaos in the courts have not been borne out, but judges have seen a steady flow of human rights cases. Of 87 decided between October and mid-February, 15 succeeded, according to figures from the human rights research unit at King's College law school, University of London. As predicted, the biggest category are claims over the right to a fair trial, guaranteed by article 6 of the Convention.

5   What does the writer imply about the outcome of Ken and Jacky Duffy's appeal against New Forest District Council?

   A   It was doomed to be a failure from the very start.

   B   It could not have been foreseen by anyone.

   C   It went against the spirit of the Human Rights Act.

   D   It opened the floodgates to other local complaints.

6   What does the writer imply about the Human Rights Act which came into force on 2 October?

   A   Too many people are taking advantage of it.

   B   Too few people have used it to claim a fair trial.

   C   It led to fear amongst those who needed it most.

   D   It was generally thought it would be abused.

Penal practice in a changing society

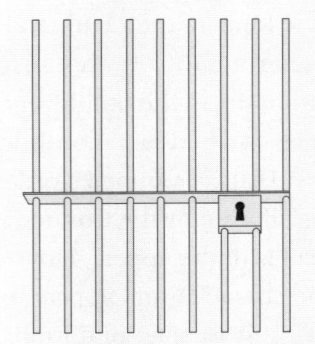

After the 1939–45 war, the Criminal Justice Act of 1948 abolished the obsolete concepts of penal servitude and hard labour. The steady rise in the prison population, and the large number of changes made during the 1950s, pointed to the need for a coherent strategy for the future. An official document 'Penal Practice in a Changing Society', published in 1959, was a major acknowledgement of this. Its aim was to prevent as many offenders as possible from returning to crime and a number of steps were outlined as to how this aim was to be pursued. It was proposed to take further the principle that prison was not a suitable place for young offenders: more detention centres would be built so that all those sentenced to a term of six months or less would be sent there, and those sentenced to between six months and three years would be taught a trade which would help them to lead a new life.

It was recognised that most local prisons were now overcrowded and conditions inside them were unsuitable. Plans for the redevelopment of local prisons were therefore included in the proposed building programme. There were also ambitious proposals for a more sophisticated observation and classification process for adult prisoners to cater for specialised needs. It was hoped that ever greater use would be made of open prisons which had expanded rapidly since the war. The first steps in this direction were taken in the early 1960s when recidivists were allocated to Ashwell open prison; previously, open conditions had generally been considered suitable mostly for first offenders.

7 According to the writer, why was the 1959 document important?

A It predicted a large number of changes in society as a whole.

B It separated young offenders from adults inside prisons.

C It aimed to cut prison sentences for young offenders to the minimum.

D It tackled the problem of prisoners who reoffended.

8 What did the proposed redevelopment plan aim to do?

A enable prison staff to operate more effectively

B build more open prisons for first offenders

C implement changes to existing local prisons

D transfer inmates of open prisons to local prisons

Paper 1 Part 3 ▶ page 70

Paper 2 Writing   Part 1

You **must** answer this question. Write your answer in **300–350** words in an appropriate style.

An international weekly news magazine is running a series of articles about guns and gun control. Read this extract from a previous article on the subject. Write an article about attitudes towards guns in your country outlining your own opinions on the subject.

> I believe passionately that we should be able to own guns if we want to. I have a rifle for target shooting at a local club, and the sport is growing rapidly in popularity. In the winter I have a shotgun and enjoy hunting in the forests. An acquaintance of mine even carries a hand gun for self-defence; so far he has never had to use it, but he says he would feel vulnerable without it.
>
> Of course, accidents will happen, and whenever they do there is a great outcry. There are calls for stricter controls or even an outright ban, but so far they have not succeeded. And the reason why is simple – guns in themselves are not dangerous; it is people who can be dangerous, and there is no way of controlling them.

Write your **article**.

Paper 2 Part 2 ▶ page 72

Paper 3 Use of English — Part 2

For questions **1–10**, read the text below. Use the word given in **capitals** at the end of some of the lines to form a word that fits in the space in the same line. There is an example at the beginning **(0)**. Write your answers **in CAPITAL LETTERS on the separate answer sheet**.

Example: **0** VANDALISM

Ancient park under threat

Pontefract Heritage Group is so concerned with the level of (0) *vandalism* at their ancient park that it has written to Council Leader Peter Box asking him to tackle the (1) .... worrying problem. In one of the most recent incidents, eight birch, ash and maple trees were sawn down. Pontefract's bowling club is planning to create an (2) .... zone by fencing off the greens to prevent further (3) .... damage to them. These attacks come hot on the heels of damage inflicted on Pontefract Castle by gangs of youths who have ripped masonry (4) .... from the ruins. Michael Holdsworth, Chairman of the Heritage group, yesterday commented:

'(5) .... damage has occurred over several years in the gardens and action taken to stop the culprits entering at night has so far been (6) .... And it's not just the bad (7) .... of teenagers which is wreaking havoc with the gardens. Adults misuse them too in the daytime by parking on the grass and flower-beds.'

Earlier this year, English Heritage gave the gardens Grade II status as a site of (8) .... interest in a national register of parks and gardens. The gardens date back to the thirteenth century, when the land formed part of the monastery gardens of Pontefract's Dominican Friary. Earning a place in the register means that the local council is required to make (9) .... for the protection of the gardens. (10) ...., this means that more investment is now needed to tackle the problems facing the gardens and provide much-needed facilities.

VANDAL
INCREASE
EXCLUDE
EXTEND
DISCRIMINATE
NOTICE
EFFECT
BEHAVE
HISTORY
PROVIDE
UNDERSTAND

Paper 3 Part 3 ▶ page 73

Paper 4 Listening   Part 2

You will hear someone talking about a new scheme for those who have broken the law. For questions **1–9**, complete the sentences with a word or short phrase.

Offenders are being given an opportunity to [1] _____ for crimes they have committed.

The [2] _____ is responsible for supervising the work of the offenders.

Because Mary Rose's bungalow was beside a [3] _____ it made her vulnerable to attack.

The schemes provide an opportunity for using the [4] _____ of the offenders.

A narrow boat project benefited those with [5] _____ in West Yorkshire.

Anyone in a [6] _____ can take a trip on the *Lady Rhodes*.

Crimes committed locally during [7] _____ have been greatly reduced.

Those previously unable to go on the waterways can now enjoy a [8] _____ on a narrow boat.

It is encouraging to think that offenders now take [9] _____ into consideration.

Paper 4 Part 3 ➡ page 75

Unit 11

Paper 1 Reading   Part 3

You are going to read an article from a newspaper. Seven paragraphs have been removed from the extract. Choose from the paragraphs **A–H** the one which fits each gap **(1–7)**. There is one extra paragraph which you do not need to use. Mark your answers **on the separate answer sheet**.

Cruising may not be everyone's idea of entertainment yet it would hardly be the same without its traditional British teatime. There is no better way of breaking down social barriers either. Or so I found when I enjoyed a cup of tea with an anonymous-looking passenger aboard the smart ship I had joined.

1

Sharing tea with a celebrity may not be a normal cruising experience, but the *Seabourn Spirit* is no run-of-the-mill vessel. Nor aboard most cruise ships are you served high-quality leaf tea – it is usually tea-bags, even if it is in a silver pot.

2

And with due reverence to the clientele, it was personal treatment all the way. With a passenger–crew ratio of almost one-to-one, there was never any chance of the delays you might experience on other craft. Nor do you find many lines where the staff are so quick and keen to learn your particular tastes.

3

In what other ship, I wonder, would the cabin stewardess put a marker in your paperback so you would not lose your place? A small detail – but little pleasures add up to give maximum satisfaction. Yet such high standards might daunt some, fearing that it will be far from relaxing having to live up to them. But I have not often been on such a happy-go-lucky cruise. Be we president or pleb, we were all treated as equals, and I have been on much less distinguished ships with more marked social mores.

4

Full silver service meals were available in your cabin as part of the 24-hour waiter service. Passengers could also choose between the main dining room and the veranda café. The cuisine was worthy of such a ship and, if it was too *nouvelle* for some, at least it made eating those cream cakes at tea less of a worry.

5

If there was any problem, it was overcoming the temptation to become a seagoing hermit. All the cabins have broad picture windows and living areas with settee, soft chairs, table and desk. And there is plenty of room for the queen-size bed. The marble bathrooms are a good size with a decent tub-shower and double wash-basins. Most convenient is a closet with enough wooden coat hangers for a débutante's ball and plenty of room for luggage.

6

A highlight of our tour was a visit to the scenic resort of Yalta and the Livadiya Palace, where Churchill, Roosevelt and Stalin held their famous conference in 1945 that decided much of the fate of post-war Europe. And we paid a rare cruise ship call to Sevastopol. Mooring near a flotilla of heavily armed warships in what is still a big naval base was one of the more thought-provoking experiences.

7

The main port brought back the smiles – a chance at last to indulge in that cruise essential, shopping, but with a touch of culture. As a mark of the special attention given to the passengers, the line booked the opera house for an exclusive ballet performance. Even if cruising is not your cup of tea, this is almost certainly the ship to change your mind.

A The passenger clearly seemed to be enjoying the occasion. During a gale, however, he might have wished he was back in port. Seasickness can afflict anyone. A good pair of sea legs is one of the few comforts not provided on a ship where every effort is made to satisfy passengers' whims.

B Yet nothing moved our emotions more than when we were driven to the site of the Valley of Death. Today, it is a sylvan scene. Had it not been for Olga, our guide, the horror of it would have remained hidden. In perfect English, she recited Tennyson's 'Charge of the Light Brigade'. I saw the American woman beside me shed a tear. She was not the only one.

C A more potent concern, even before boarding, was not over-eating but over-drinking. One reason for such high fares is that drinks are included without extra charge. But the mainly elderly passengers stayed as sober as judges – as several were, in fact.

D Although under 10,000 tons, a midget of the ocean waves, what it lacks in size it makes up for in quality. 'Luxury' is a much abused word, yet this ship deserves the description. 'Exclusive' may be a better word if you reckon on the ability to pay an average of more than £550 a day for the pleasure of being there. It was not surprising, therefore, that the majority of the 188 passengers on our 12-night jaunt from Istanbul to the Black Sea and Aegean came from the richer golden lodes of the social strata.

E My fridge, too, was stocked to the gunnels. As another compulsion to remain in blissful isolation, the television also relays the ship's daily lectures on port news and travel subjects. There were half a dozen grander suites with separate rooms and a balcony. If you could tear yourself away from the room or felt like a more academic pastime, the ship also had its own library, but it would take a world cruise at least to read through the edition of *Encyclopaedia Britannica* that was included.

F Nothing boosts egos more, or makes one feel more at home, than having the steward know without being reminded that your breakfast croissants should be only slightly warm and that you prefer Orange Pekoe to Darjeeling.

G Sipping from his cup English-style (with milk) with obvious pleasure, he told me: 'I enjoy it very much although we do grow excellent tea in my country, Indonesia. It's called Gol Para. Did you know that it is a favourite kind of your Queen?' This surprised me but then who am I to dispute a former president of his country?

H Just to illustrate my point: aboard Seabourn Spirit, there were just three formal dinners, and not all the men wore dinner jackets. Most evenings were casual or informal.

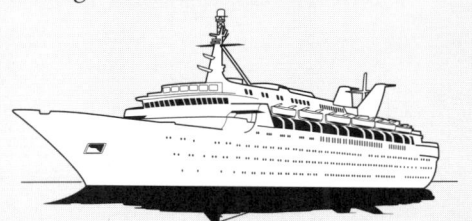

Paper 1 Part 4 ▶ page 76

Paper 2 Writing   Part 2

Write an answer to **one** of the questions **1–3** in this part. Write your answer in **300–350** words in an appropriate style.

1   A literary magazine is publishing a series of articles about the portrayal of the generation gap in films and books. Write a review of a book or film you know well, commenting on the relationship between two characters from different generations and outlining how significant this is to the story as a whole.

   Write your **review**.

2   You are on the committee of a film club, and you have been selected to write a proposal to the local council asking for funds to hold a film festival. In your proposal you should outline your reasons for holding the festival, the kind of films you would show, and the benefits that the festival would bring.

   Write your **proposal**.

3   A national newspaper has been running a series of stories about the balance between civil liberties and greater police powers. Write a letter to the paper giving your views, outlining the extent to which you think the average citizen would benefit or suffer from a reduction in civil liberties.

   Write your **letter**.

Paper 3 Use of English   Part 3

For questions **1–6**, think of **one** word only which can be used appropriately in all three sentences. Here is an example **(0)**.

Example:

0   The committee is totally against any new building in a .... belt area.

When Frank saw Sally's new car, he was .... with envy.

I obviously haven't got .... fingers because I can't get anything to grow.

Example: | 0 | G | R | E | E | N | | | | | | | | | | |

Write only the missing word **in CAPITAL LETTERS on the separate answer sheet**.

---

1   Watch your .... here because the floor's very slippery!

We need to deal with this matter taking one .... at a time.

With every .... the soldier felt weaker.

2   As midnight approached, the guests slowly .... away from the party.

Overnight, the snow had .... into great piles up against the garden wall.

My thoughts .... back to the days when I believed everything was possible.

3   The draught from the windows always seems to .... out the candles in the dining room.

Could you help me .... up these balloons for Tim's party?

If you don't stop switching the lights on and off, you'll .... a fuse!

4 The robberies seem to follow a similar …………………… of events.

Cut round the edges of the dress …………………… , then stitch the seams of the material together.

The curtain material has an attractive …………………… of circles and stars.

5 Our local football team has been trying to get into the first …………………… for the last two years.

Tim is no good at long …………………… , but he's brilliant at multiplication.

The seemingly unfair …………………… of wealth seems to be balanced in favour of those who have been well educated.

6 For this activity, it is advisable to …………………… the class into three groups.

The best way to …………………… the logs is with an axe.

The managing director decided to …………………… the difference between the two proposed prices for the new product.

Paper 3 Part 4 ▶ page 78

Paper 4 Listening   Part 3

You will hear an interview with Owen Jackson, who is talking about his work as a film director. For questions **1–5**, choose the answer (**A**, **B**, **C** or **D**) which fits best according to what you hear.

1 Owen says that the film which made him successful

  A was finished long before the 1990s.
  B was rejected by the industry when it first came out.
  C overran its original budget.
  D was made in very difficult conditions.

2 What motivated Owen to make the film in Australia?

  A a desire to be accepted into the Hollywood system
  B a feeling that his next movie would be a winner
  C a determination to do what he wanted to do
  D a fear that this might be his last chance to prove himself

3 According to Owen, what made his film *Task Force* unusual?

  A Genuine soldiers were brought in as actors.
  B The cast were put through rigorous training.
  C Filming took months longer than anticipated.
  D Owen based the characters on fellow soldiers.

4 What does Owen feel about all films?

  A They are part of an evolutionary process.
  B They are significant landmarks.
  C They are rarely regarded as highly as they should be.
  D They are regarded with envy by fellow directors.

5 What does Owen say about the future?

  A World events will always dictate how we perceive ourselves.
  B Turmoil will continue unless we make a stand.
  C People should not try to reproduce what he has created on film.
  D We can be optimistic about the human race.

Paper 4 Part 4 ▶ page 82

Unit 12

Paper 1 Reading   Part 4

You are going to read an article about the escapologist, Harry Houdini. For questions 1–7, choose the answer (**A**, **B**, **C** or **D**) which you think fits best according to the text. Mark your answers **on the separate answer sheet**.

Mind over matter?

Harry Houdini, who died in 1927, was the entertainment phenomenon of the ragtime era. He could escape from chains and padlocks, from ropes and canvas sacks. They put him in a strait-jacket and hung him upside down from a skyscraper and he somehow untied himself. They tied him up in a locked packing case and sank him in Liverpool docks. Minutes later he surfaced smiling. They locked him in a zinc-lined Russian prison van and he emerged leaving the doors locked and the locks undamaged. They padlocked him in a milk churn full of water and he burst free. They put him in a coffin, screwed down the lid, and buried him and ... well, no, he didn't pop up like a mole, but when they dug him up more than half an hour later, he was still breathing.

Houdini would usually allow his equipment to be examined by the audience. The chains, locks and packing cases all seemed perfectly genuine, so it was tempting to conclude that he possessed superhuman powers. Sir Arthur Conan Doyle's Sherlock Holmes was the very paragon of analytical thinking but Conan Doyle believed that Houdini achieved his tricks through spiritualism. Indeed, he wrote to the escapologist imploring him to use his psychic powers more profitably for the common good instead of just prostituting his talent every night at the Alhambra. However, Houdini repeatedly denounced spiritualism and disclaimed any psychic element to his act.

The alternative explanation for his feats of escapism was that Houdini could do unnatural things with his body. It is widely held that he could dislocate his shoulders to escape from strait-jackets, and that he could somehow contract his wrists in order to escape from handcuffs. His ability to spend long periods in confined spaces is cited as evidence that he could put his body into suspended animation, as Indian fakirs are supposed to do.

This is all nonsense. If you ever find yourself in a strait-jacket, it's difficult to imagine anything less helpful than a dislocated shoulder. Contracting your wrists is not only unhelpful but, frankly, impossible because the bones of your wrist are very tightly packed together and the whole structure is virtually incompressible. As for suspended animation, the trick of surviving burial and drowning relies on the fact that you can live for short periods on the air in a confined space. The air shifted by an average person in a day would occupy a cube just eight feet square. The build-up of carbon monoxide tends to pollute this supply, but, if you can relax, the air in a coffin should keep you going for half an hour or so.

In other words, there was nothing physically remarkable about Houdini except for his bravery, dexterity and fitness. His nerve was so cool that he could remain in a coffin six feet underground until they came to dig him up. His fingers were so strong that he could undo a buckle or manipulate keys through the canvas of a strait-jacket or a mail bag. He made a comprehensive study of locks and was able to conceal lock-picks about his person in a way which fooled even the doctors who examined him. When they locked him in the prison van he still had a hacksaw blade with which to saw through the joins in the metal lining and get access to the planks of the floor. As an entertainer he combined all this strength and ingenuity with a lot of trickery. His stage escapes took place behind a curtain with an orchestra playing to disguise the banging and sawing. The milk churn in which he was locked had a double lining so that, while the lid was locked onto the rim, the rim was not actually attached to the churn. Houdini merely had to stand up to get out. The mail sack he cut open at the seam and sewed up with similar thread. The bank safe from which he emerged had been secretly worked on by his mechanics for 24 hours before the performance.

All Houdini's feats are eminently explicable, although to explain them, even now, is a kind of heresy. Houdini belongs to that band of mythical supermen who, we like to believe, were capable of miracles and would still be alive today were it not for some piece of low trickery. It's said of Houdini that a punch in his belly when he wasn't prepared for it caused his burst appendix. Anatomically, it's virtually impossible that a punch could puncture your gut, but the story endures. Somehow the myth of the superman has an even greater appeal than the edifice of twenty-first century logic.

1 In the first paragraph, what does the writer say Houdini managed to do?

  A jump upside down from a skyscraper

  B escape from a submerged box

  C break the locks of a Russian prison van

  D fight his way out of an empty milk churn

2 The writer mentions Houdini's burial alive to illustrate the fact that

  A his tricks sometimes went disastrously wrong.

  B he was not always able to do what he claimed he could.

  C he was capable of extraordinary feats of survival.

  D he had overcome his fear of confined spaces.

3 The writer suggests that Conan Doyle

  A was less analytical about Houdini than one might have expected.

  B asked Houdini if he could include him in a Sherlock Holmes story.

  C felt that Houdini could make more money in other ways.

  D thought there were scientific explanations for Houdini's feats.

4 The writer comes to the conclusion that Houdini

  A had an unusual bone structure.

  B could make parts of his body smaller.

  C was able to put himself in a trance.

  D was not physically abnormal.

5 It appears that Houdini was able to escape from strait-jackets by

  A using hidden lock-picks.

  B undoing buckles from inside the material.

  C cutting the canvas with a hacksaw.

  D turning keys he had concealed.

6 The writer states that when Houdini escaped from the milk churn

  A the role of the orchestra was important.

  B he made use of the hacksaw to free himself.

  C the container had been modified beforehand.

  D he was in full sight of the audience.

7 How does the writer say people regard Houdini nowadays?

  A They want to hear the scientific explanations for his feats.

  B They prefer to believe that he had extraordinary powers.

  C They refuse to believe the story of how he died.

  D They doubt the fact that he ever really existed.

Paper 3 Use of English   Part 4

For questions **1–8**, complete the second sentence so that it has a similar meaning to the first sentence, using the word given. **Do not change the word given.** You must use between **three** and **eight** words, including the word given. Here is an example **(0)**.

Example:

0   You ran the risk of being burgled when you left the door unlocked.

broken

Your house …................................…... when you left the door unlocked.

0	could have been broken into

Write only the missing words on the separate answer sheet.

1   I regret agreeing to do the extra work.

on

If only ……………………………………………. the extra work.

2   We were sorry that we did not get our examination results until after the end of term.

through

We wish our examination results ……………………………………………… the end of term.

3   It's too late to try and phone them now.

point

It's so late that there ……………………………………………. phone them now.

4 The alarm went off just as they came out of the building.

when

Scarcely ………………………………………………… the alarm went off.

5 No one listened to what the politician was saying last night.

ears

What the politician was saying ………………………………………………… last night.

6 Some improvements will have to have to be made if you all want to pass this exam.

socks

You will all ………………………………………………… if you want to pass this exam.

7 This medicine will relieve the pain, but it will not cure everything.

miracles

This medicine ………………………………………………… bring some pain relief.

8 Who disagrees with our intention to go on strike?

favour

Is there anyone ………………………………………………… our going on strike?

Paper 3 Part 5 ▶ page 80

Paper 3 Use of English   Part 5

For questions **1–5**, read the following texts on artificial intelligence. For questions **1–4**, answer with a word or short phrase. You do not need to write complete sentences. For question **5**, write a summary according to the instructions given. Write your answers to questions **1–5 on the separate answer sheet**.

line 2

The problem with computers is that stripped of their mystique and dazzling accessories, at present they are nothing more than glorified adding machines. While they can be modified to become word processors, at their core they are still adding machines. They can manipulate vast amounts of data millions of times faster than humans, but they do not understand what they are doing and have no independent thought. Nor can they program themselves.

One of the principal problems in the future will be to build intelligent systems with common sense. Like the huge concealed portion of an iceberg hidden beneath the waves, common sense is so embedded in our brains at such an unconscious level that we don't even ponder how we use it in our daily lives. Only the tiniest fraction of our thinking is devoted to conscious thought.

Ironically, our brains never evolved the remarkably simple neural circuits it takes to do arithmetic. Being able to multiply five-digit numbers, which is effortlessly performed by handheld calculators, was of no use in escaping a hungry sabre-toothed tiger hundreds of thousands of years ago. Our brains did, however, evolve the sophisticated mental apparatus that enables us to understand common sense without thinking about it and survive in a hostile world.

Computer systems are the opposite; they are marvellous at abstract mathematical logic, but in general they do not grasp the simplest concepts of physics or biology.

1   What point is the writer making by using the expression 'glorified adding machines' in line 2?

....

2   Which word in paragraph 3 highlights the precarious environment humans evolved in?

....

line 2 Douglas Lenat has devoted a lifetime to conquering the mysteries of common sense. He feels that the problem is that artificial intelligence (AI) researchers have tiptoed around the periphery of the real problem. His challenge is to create an Encyclopaedia of Common Sense, i.e. a nearly complete set of common-sense rules. In other words, instead of analysing isolated pieces of logic, he is advocating a brute force, take-no-prisoners approach.

Lenat believes that in the future everyone will load common-sense programs into their computers, allowing them to have intelligent conversations with their computers, which will be capable of interpreting and carrying out people's commands. At times, however, Lenat despairs of compiling all the ambiguities hidden within the English language, ambiguities which are only resolved by a person's knowledge of the real world. Take, for example, the statement: 'Mary saw a bicycle in the store window. She wanted it.' Lenat says, 'How do we know that she wanted the bicycle, and not the store, or the window?' The actual resolution of this simple problem requires the program to understand the nearly complete set of likes and dislikes of human beings.

One of Lenat's intermediate goals is to hit the 'break even' point, where the computer will be able to learn faster by simply 'reading' new material, rather than by having an army of tutors with Ph.Ds. Like a young bird taking off on its maiden flight, it will then be able to soar on its own power. At that point, it can dispense with human teachers and, like a ten-year-old child, read and learn on its own.

3 Explain in your own words why the writer has chosen to use the word 'tiptoed' in line 2.

....

4 Which word in paragraph 3 develops the simile of the young bird?

....

5 In a paragraph of between **50 and 70** words, summarise **in your own words as far as possible**, the limitations of artificial intelligence as outlined in the texts. Write your summary **on the separate answer sheet**.

Paper 4 Listening   Part 4

You will hear two psychologists, Tim and Juliet, talking on the radio about the abilities of the human brain. For questions **1–6**, decide whether the opinions are expressed by only one of the speakers, or whether the speakers agree.

Write   **T**   for Tim,
        J   for Juliet,
or   **B**   for Both, where they agree.

---

1   The human brain's ability is not restricted to one type of knowledge.

2   An inability to cope with mathematics could be due to a lack of encouragement from others.

3   Everyone's brain is constantly doing mathematical calculations.

4   Using something to direct your eyes towards figures can improve your mathematical ability.

5   Keeping silent and focusing carefully on the numbers is a tricky technique to perfect.

6   Scoring is not advisable in mathematical games.

Sample Speaking Test

1 General information

You take the revised CPE Paper 5 Speaking in pairs, although you may find yourself in a group of three if there is an unpaired candidate at the end of the examining session. There are two examiners: the Interlocutor, who conducts the test, and the Assessor who takes no active part in the test.

2 Test focus

Part 1 focuses on general interaction and social language.

Part 2 focuses on speculating, evaluating, comparing, giving opinions, decision-making, collaborating, etc.

Part 3 focuses on organising speech coherently, making relevant contributions, expressing and justifying opinions, and developing topics.

3 Marking

You are assessed throughout the test on your own performance and not in relation to each other. The Assessor awards a mark of between 0 and 5 for each of the categories below. A score of 3 is regarded as an adequate performance mark for a Grade C.

Assessment categories	Main focus
Grammatical resource	*accuracy, range and appropriate use*
Lexical resource	*range and appropriateness*
Discourse management	*coherence, extent and relevance*
Pronunciation	*stress and rhythm, intonation and individual sounds*
Interactive communication	*initiating and responding, avoiding undue hesitation, and turn-taking*
Global mark	
Global achievement	*This is an impression mark based on overall performance.*

4 Predicting and analysing performance

You will hear some CPE students taking part in a Speaking Test. For each part of the test, answer the prediction questions, then listen to the recording and answer the analysis questions.

Part One (3 minutes)

Prediction Here are some examples of Part One questions. What answers would you give to these questions?

- *Are you a student or do you work? Could you tell us something about it?*
- *Can you describe how you spend your leisure time?*
- *If you could study another language apart from English, which one would you choose?*
- *What job skills do you think people will need in the future?*

Analysis Now listen to Silvia and Andrea doing Part 1 of the test and answer these questions.

1 How do the students cope with the examiner's questions in the three different sections of Part 1?

2 Is their performance different from what you expected?

Part Two (4 minutes) Local Environment Campaign

The first task (1 minute)

Prediction Look at pictures A and B on page 90 and read the task below. What do you think might have motivated the people in pictures A and B?

Here are some pictures of measures being taken to improve the environment. First, look at pictures A and B and talk together about what you think might have motivated the people to do these things.

Analysis Now listen to Silvia and Andrea doing the first section of Part 2 of the test and answer these questions.

1 Do the students do what the examiner asks them to?

2 How different were the students' responses from your own?

The second task (3 minutes)

Prediction Look at all four pictures on page 90 and read the task below. How do you think environmental problems are being addressed in each photo? Can you think of two other images to promote the campaign?

Now, look at all the pictures. Imagine that your local council is running a campaign to improve the environment in the city where you live. These photographs will be used to promote some of their ideas. Talk about how environmental problems are being addressed in each photo, then suggest two other images you would use to promote the campaign.

Analysis Now listen to the students doing the second section of Part 2 of the test and answer these questions.

1 Do the students do what the examiner asks them to?
2 What techniques do they use to maintain the interaction?

Part Three (12 minutes) Media access

Two-minute talk

Prediction Look at prompt card A. Take ten seconds to think of some ideas and make notes.

Prompt Card A

> **What effects has TV had on our lives?**
>
> ➢ **access to information**
> ➢ **family relationships**
> ➢ **outdoor activities**

Analysis Now listen to Natalie giving her two-minute talk and Caroline commenting on what she has said and answer these questions.

1 How do Natalie's ideas compare with yours?
2 How does Natalie organise the information in her talk?
3 What extra ideas does Caroline add?

Theme-related questions

Prediction Look at some of the theme-related questions the students were asked.

Which of the questions do you think might be the hardest to answer? What would your answers be?

- *In what way can watching violent programmes or films affect people's behaviour?*
- *How far does the media raise our expectations in life?*
- *To what extent should advertising in the media be controlled?*
- *Which do you consider to be more influential: the written or the spoken word?*

Analysis

A Listen to Muriel and Xavier answering a question in Part 3 of the test and answer these questions.

1 What unexpected angle to the question do the students introduce?
2 How effective is this analogy in getting their points of view across?

B Listen to Marina and Silvia answering another question in Part 3 of the test and answer these questions.

1 What problem do the students have with this question?
2 What is the best way to deal with this kind of situation in a Speaking Test?

C Now listen to Natalie and Caroline answering the questions *To what extent should advertising in the media be controlled?* and *Which do you consider to be more influential: the written or the spoken word?* in Part 3 of the test. Answer these questions.

1 How do the students cope with these two questions?
2 Are their answers different from what yours would have been?

5 Practice

Now it's your turn. Find two partners to practise the different parts of the test.

Part One

In groups of three, Student A assumes the role of the examiner and asks the other students some of the questions.

Hint

Don't give a one-word answer. Try to extend your answers and give more relevant information where appropriate.

Part One (3 minutes)

Examiner	Good morning. My name is … And your names are…?
Students' replies	………………………………..
Examiner	Thank you. Now, first of all, it would be nice to find out something about each of you. Where are you from (*Student A*)? And you (*Student B*)?
	Choose one question for each student.
	Do you live in the city centre?
	How do you travel to school?
	What do you dislike about living here?
	How long did it take you to get here this morning?
Students' replies	………………………………..
Examiner	*Choose one question for each student.*
	Are you a student or do you work? Could you tell us something about it?
	Could you tell us what you remember most about your childhood?
	Can you describe how you spend your leisure time?
	Could you tell us the main reasons why you are learning English?
	Can you say what you hope to do in the future?
Students' replies	………………………………..
Examiner	*Choose one more question for each student.*
	If you could study another language apart from English, which one would you choose? Why?
	What job skills do you think people will need in the future?
	How well do you think your education has prepared you for your future life?
	How important do you think it is to be ambitious in life?
Students' replies	………………………………..
Examiner	Thank you.

Sample Speaking Test

> **Hint**
> Remember to invite your partner to take part in the conversation. Make an active contribution yourself but do not try to dominate the conversation.

Part Two

In groups of three, Student B assumes the role of the examiner.

Use the pictures on page 87 to do the task.

Part Two (4 minutes) Local Environment Campaign

Examiner	Here are some pictures of measures being taken to improve the environment.
	First, I'd like you to look at pictures A and B and talk together about what you think might have motivated the people to do these things.
Students' replies ⏲ *1 minute*	....
Examiner	Thank you. Now, I'd like you to look at all the pictures.
	I'd like you to imagine that your local council is running a campaign to improve the environment in the city where you live. These photographs will be used to promote some of their ideas.
	Talk together about how environmental problems are being addressed in each photo, then suggest two other images you would use to promote the campaign.
Students' replies ⏲ *3 minutes*	....
Examiner	Thank you.

> **Hint**
> Don't simply describe the pictures. You have only a minute for this, so concentrate on the speculative aspect of the task.

> **Hint**
> Do what the examiner asks you to do but don't forget to make suggestions for two images of your own.

Page 86

Sample Speaking Test

| A | B |
| C | D |

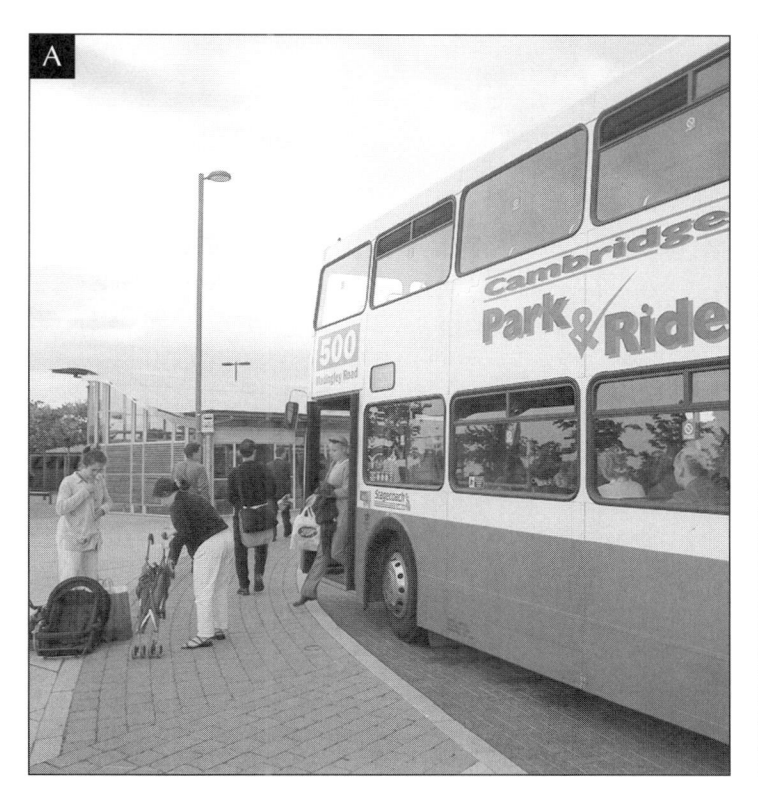

Sample Speaking Test

Page 87

Part Three

Two-minute talk

In groups of three, Student C assumes the role of the examiner.

Use the prompt cards below.

Part Three (12 minutes) Media access

Examiner	Now, in this part of the test you're each going to talk on your own for about two minutes. You need to listen while your partner is speaking because you'll be asked to comment afterwards.
[A]	So (*Student A*), I'm going to give you a card with a question written on it and I'd like you to tell us what you think. There are also some ideas on the card for you to use if you like. All right? Here is your card, and a copy for you (*Student B*).

Prompt Card A

> **What threats does the world face today?**
> - **changing climatic conditions**
> - **disappearance of natural resources**
> - **relations between nations**

> **Hint**
> Remember to think about the prompts on a personal, local and international level. This will help you to generate ideas.

	Remember (*Student A*), you have about two minutes to talk before we join in. [*Allow up to 10 seconds before saying, if necessary:* Would you like to begin now?]
Student A 🕒 (2 minutes)	……………………………………………………..
Examiner	Thank you *Ask Student B:* Is there anything you don't agree with?
Student B 🕒 (up to 1 minute)	………………………………………………………
Examiner	*Ask the following question to both students.* What can we do to help preserve the world's natural resources?
Students' replies 🕒 (1 minute)	…………………………………………………….
Examiner	Thank you.
Examiner	Now, (*Student B*), it's your turn to be given a question.
[B]	Here is your card, and a copy for you (*Student A*). Remember (*Student B*), you have about two minutes to tell us what you think, and there are some ideas on the card for you to use if you like. All right?

> **Hint**
> It is important to listen while your partner is speaking because you will be asked to comment on what he/she says.

Prompt Card B

> In what ways is life safer than it used to be?
> - medical care
> - safety at home and in the workplace
> - technological advances

	[*Allow up to 10 seconds before saying, if necessary:* Would you like to begin now?]
Student B ⏲ *2 minutes*	……………………………………………………..
Examiner	Thank you *Ask Student A:* Is there anything you would like to add?
Student A ⏲ *up to 1 minute*	……………………………………………………
Examiner	*Ask the following question to both students.* What technological advance do you consider has resulted in the greatest improvement in our lives in the last century?
Student's replies ⏲ *1 minute*	………………………………………………..
Examiner	Thank you.

Part 3

Theme-related questions

In groups of three, Student A assumes the role of the examiner.

Use the questions below.

Examiner	Now, to finish the test, we're going to talk about the future of the world in general. *Ask students the following questions.*
⏲ *(4 minutes)*	
	What role will money play in the world in the future? What can individuals do to help look after the world we live in? To what extent do you think the world is at risk from life on other planets? Are you optimistic or pessimistic about the future of the human race? Why?
Examiner	Thank you. That is the end of the test.

Hint

Even if you have never thought about the issues involved in the question you are asked, try to answer to the best of your ability.

Sample Speaking Test

Sample Speaking Test

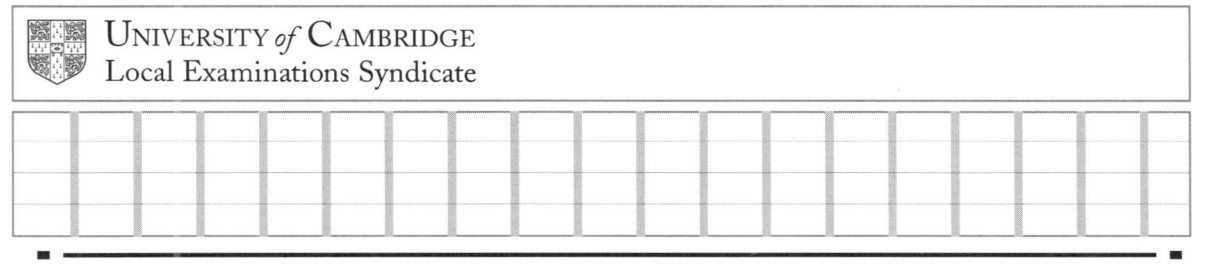

UNIVERSITY of CAMBRIDGE
Local Examinations Syndicate

Candidate Name
If not already printed, write name in CAPITALS and complete the Candidate No. grid (in pencil).

Candidate's Signature

Examination Title

Centre

Supervisor:
If the candidate is ABSENT or has WITHDRAWN shade here

Centre No.

Candidate No.

Examination Details

Candidate Answer Sheet

Instructions
Use a soft PENCIL (B or HB).

Mark ONE letter only for each question.

For example, if you think B is the right answer, mark your answer sheet like this:

0 A B C D

Rub out any answer you wish to change.

Part 1
1 A B C D
2 A B C D
3 A B C D
4 A B C D
5 A B C D
6 A B C D
7 A B C D
8 A B C D
9 A B C D
10 A B C D
11 A B C D
12 A B C D
13 A B C D
14 A B C D
15 A B C D
16 A B C D
17 A B C D
18 A B C D

Part 2
19 A B C D
20 A B C D
21 A B C D
22 A B C D
23 A B C D
24 A B C D
25 A B C D
26 A B C D

Part 4
34 A B C D
35 A B C D
36 A B C D
37 A B C D
38 A B C D
39 A B C D
40 A B C D

Part 3
27 A B C D E F G H
28 A B C D E F G H
29 A B C D E F G H
30 A B C D E F G H
31 A B C D E F G H
32 A B C D E F G H
33 A B C D E F G H

CPE 1   DP999/999

PHOTOCOPIABLE Taken from the revised CPE handbook © UCLES 2001

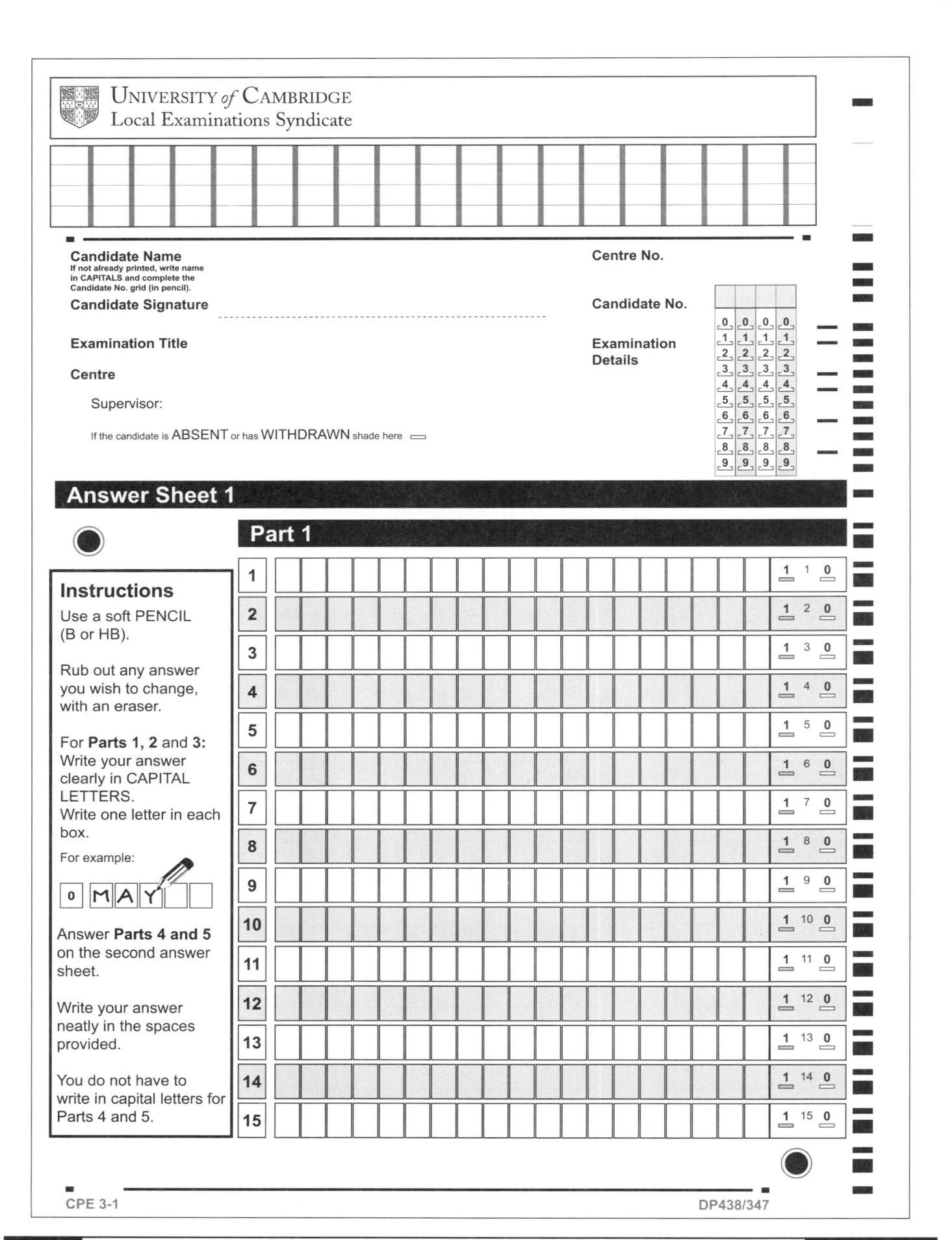

UNIVERSITY of CAMBRIDGE
Local Examinations Syndicate

Candidate Name
If not already printed, write name in CAPITALS and complete the Candidate No. grid (in pencil).

Candidate Signature

Examination Title

Centre

Supervisor:

If the candidate is ABSENT or has WITHDRAWN shade here

Centre No.

Candidate No.

Examination Details

Answer Sheet 1

Part 1

Instructions

Use a soft PENCIL (B or HB).

Rub out any answer you wish to change, with an eraser.

For **Parts 1, 2** and **3**:
Write your answer clearly in CAPITAL LETTERS.
Write one letter in each box.

For example:

| 0 | M | A | Y | | |

Answer **Parts 4 and 5** on the second answer sheet.

Write your answer neatly in the spaces provided.

You do not have to write in capital letters for Parts 4 and 5.

CPE 3-1

DP438/347

Part 2

16	
17	
18	
19	
20	
21	
22	
23	
24	
25	

Part 3

26	
27	
28	
29	
30	
31	

Continue with Parts 4 and 5 on Answer Sheet 2 ▶

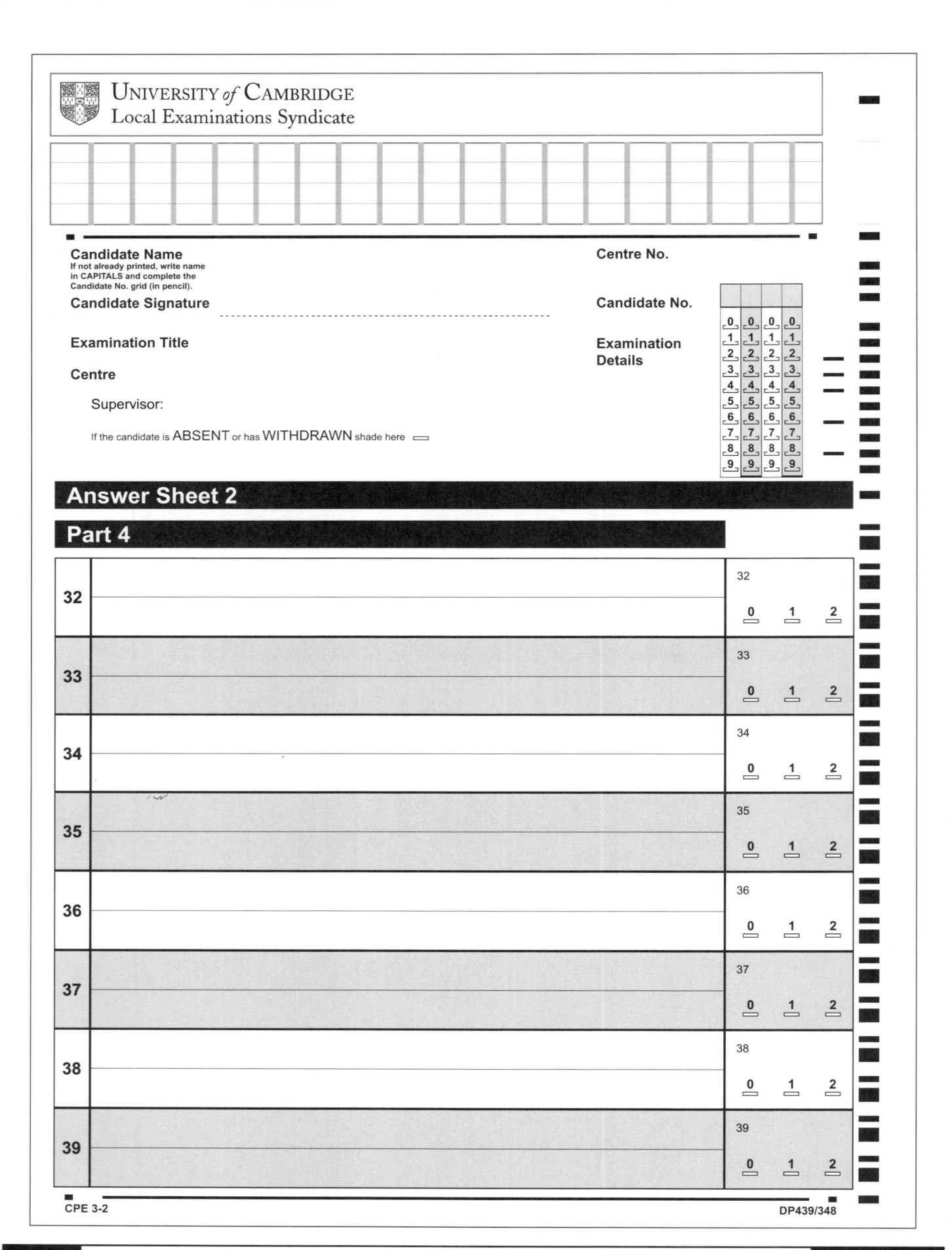

UNIVERSITY of CAMBRIDGE
Local Examinations Syndicate

Candidate Name
If not already printed, write name in CAPITALS and complete the Candidate No. grid (in pencil).

Candidate Signature

Examination Title

Centre

Supervisor:

If the candidate is ABSENT or has WITHDRAWN shade here ▭

Centre No.

Candidate No.

Examination Details

Answer Sheet 2

Part 4

Q	Answer	Marks
32		0 1 2
33		0 1 2
34		0 1 2
35		0 1 2
36		0 1 2
37		0 1 2
38		0 1 2
39		0 1 2

CPE 3-2

DP439/348

Part 5

40		40 0 1 2
41		41 0 1 2
42		42 0 1 2
43		43 0 1 2

Part 5: question 44

For Examiner use only

Marks

Content	0 1 2 3 4
Language	0 1.1 1.2 2.1 2.2 3.1 3.2 4.1 4.2 5.1 5.2

Examiner number: Team and Position

PHOTOCOPIABLE   Taken from the revised CPE handbook © UCLES 2001   Page 95

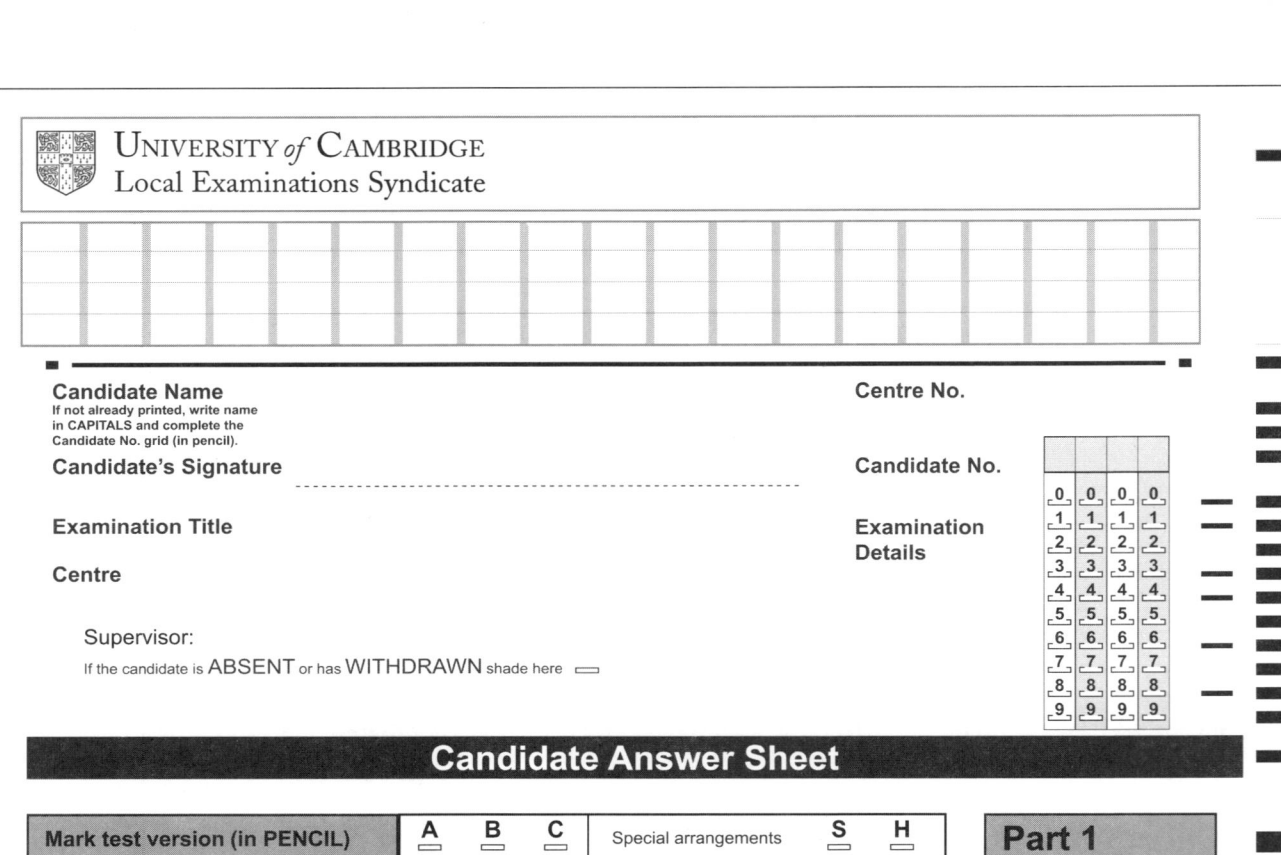

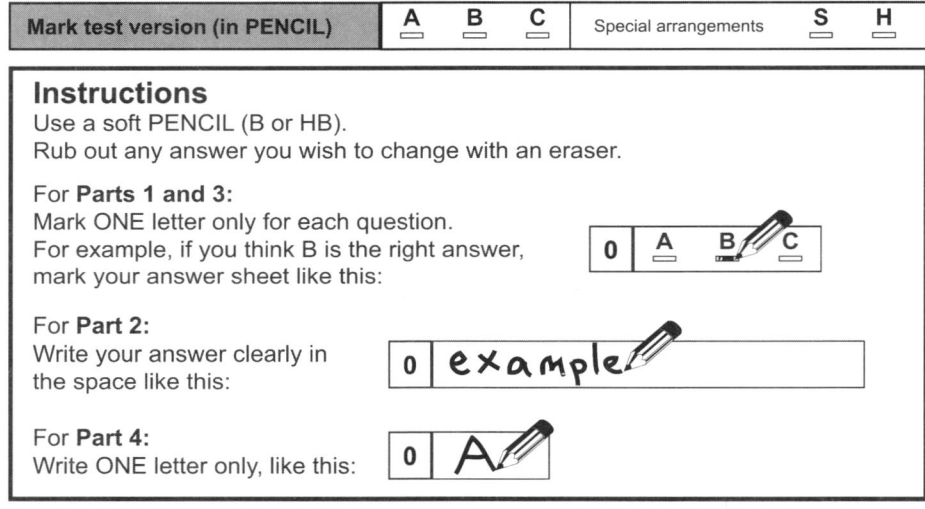

UNIVERSITY of CAMBRIDGE
Local Examinations Syndicate

Candidate Name
If not already printed, write name in CAPITALS and complete the Candidate No. grid (in pencil).

Candidate's Signature

Examination Title

Centre

Supervisor:
If the candidate is ABSENT or has WITHDRAWN shade here ▭

Centre No.

Candidate No.

Examination Details

Candidate Answer Sheet

Mark test version (in PENCIL) A B C   **Special arrangements** S H

Instructions
Use a soft PENCIL (B or HB).
Rub out any answer you wish to change with an eraser.

For **Parts 1 and 3**:
Mark ONE letter only for each question.
For example, if you think B is the right answer, mark your answer sheet like this:

0 A B C

For **Part 2**:
Write your answer clearly in the space like this:

0 example

For **Part 4**:
Write ONE letter only, like this:

0 A

Part 1
1	A	B	C
2	A	B	C
3	A	B	C
4	A	B	C
5	A	B	C
6	A	B	C
7	A	B	C
8	A	B	C

Part 2
		Do not write here
9		1 9 0
10		1 10 0
11		1 11 0
12		1 12 0
13		1 13 0
14		1 14 0
15		1 15 0
16		1 16 0
17		1 17 0

Part 3
18	A	B	C	D
19	A	B	C	D
20	A	B	C	D
21	A	B	C	D
22	A	B	C	D

Part 4
		Do not write here
23		1 23 0
24		1 24 0
25		1 25 0
26		1 26 0
27		1 27 0
28		1 28 0

CPE 4
DP999/999